GOD HEARS
My Heart

LEARN HOW GOD WILL MEET YOU IN EVERYDAY LIFE.

GOD HEARS
My Heart

CAROL J. GERMAN

All scripture references in this book come from the New Living Translation (NLT).

Biblical commentary used in this book comes from *The Bible
Knowledge Commentary: An Exposition of the Scriptures* by Dallas Semi-
nary Faculty along with general editors John F. Walvoord and Roy B. Zuck.
Both Old Testament and New Testament books were used. Commentary
was used mostly in the section Understanding the Book of Revelation, at the
end of the book.

First Edition

ISBN: 978-1-952976-11-7
LOC: 2021902590

First Printing March, 2021
Cover and Interior design by: Kirk House Publishers
Krista Reynolds Photography – author head shot

Kirk House Publishers
1250 E 115th Street
Burnsville, MN 55337
612-781-2815

To my husband, Rob, who has taught me to love unconditionally.
You keep me humble and grounded.
You know how to make me laugh,
and you are the hardest working man I know.
After we got married,
you told me that I would be safe with you.
You have kept your promise.
I love you.

TABLE OF CONTENTS

MY PRAYER FOR YOU

What do you see when you look in the mirror? You may have a hard time believing that God loves you, like I did, but I am hoping that that will change after you read this book. God hears you, sees you, and has a love for you that will transform you from the inside out. My prayer is that you will be able to look in the mirror and know for certain who you belong to and who you are.

He never turns away from a heart that seeks Him. There is

Nothing would delight God more than for you to discover Him. He is your true love.

nothing you could do that would change how he feels about you. He met me, and He will meet you, right in the middle of everyday life. He has time for you, and He won't be deterred by any dark secrets or feelings of ineptness; no matter what you have locked deep inside your heart. He is passionately committed to you. He is on a mission to win you over through His love.

While I don't have formal training in theology, I write from everyday life. I simply chose to look up with a willing heart, to hear and see something beyond myself. What I discovered is that there is a God—the One and only God—who answered me *beyond my wildest dreams*. May my journey help you to find God in your own deep and transformative way.

I explain the story of God's love by using my life journey as the backdrop. You will see how God was with me through it all. You will have a clear understanding of who God is and what your part is in His love story of redemption. You will learn many nuggets of truth that will aid in walking moment by moment with God.

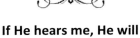

If He hears me, He will hear you, and He will reveal Himself to you. I promise.

What has inspired me to write my story is the undeniable fact that God has never left my side and that He confirms Himself to me personally on a daily basis. He has convinced me of His faithfulness and unconditional love.

At the end of the book, you will find questions from each chapter to help deepen your faith. I encourage you to take the time to answer them. The more you engage in something, the more you learn and know. The greatest skill you can gain is to learn to discern God's voice. He wants to share Himself with you in a way so that you will come to know His presence and not doubt that He is the Lover of your soul.

We begin by understanding how we need each other. I need you, you need me, and we need God. Together we are strong and united, all seven-plus billion of us. Despite any uncertainties we face, God is in control. Let's learn together how His love is faithful, enduring, and unconditional.

Before we move on, I want to share one of my earliest recollections of how God made Himself real to me. It changed me forever.

GOD HEARS MY HEART

I remember a day many years ago, after my husband, Rob, and I had purchased our first home. While we settled into married life, we faced many challenges that disrupted our wedded bliss. We entered marriage with high expectations, but we also had lots of baggage. In the coming chapters, I will share more in detail about this and about how God led us through to enduring love.

On this particular day, we were at odds. Thinking back, I can't remember exactly why, but all I know is that I was tired—tired of not being in sync. Rob's mechanism to escape from our issues was yard work, mine was cleaning the house. We both magically had chores that we needed to take care of because we didn't know how to communicate properly. So, we hid. We hid behind whatever would distract us from each other. While Rob was out mowing the grass, I sat down on the couch and read my Bible instead of cleaning. I found myself in the book of Isaiah.

While reading Isaiah 41, I read verse 10 out loud, "Do not be afraid. For I am with you. Do not be afraid, for I am your God. I will strengthen you. I will help you and I will uphold you with my victorious right hand." Something was different in that moment. I was not alone in the room. I wasn't simply reading words on a page from a book either. *I was in the presence of Christ.* I felt His presence behind me.

It was in this moment that I understood the realness of the Bible. I saw just how close God is, and how personal He was with me. God met me in the dark where no one can possibly see or understand but Him. From that moment on, I looked at the scriptures differently. This caused me to look at God differently. He gave me a desire for truth, His truth. Within the pages of the Bible, not only did I come to an understanding of who God is and how sin affects me, *I discovered the presence of Christ.*

Ever since those early days, I have found God to always be faithful to me. Even in my loneliest moments, when I look up, He is there. When I am grumbling and ranting over something, whether life-changing or miniscule, He remains by my side. In fear, He reassures me that I am courageous and strong because His presence is within me. He makes me capable of handling whatever life throws at me.

Jesus placed His hands on my shoulders, leaned down, and spoke His words to me. He read to me instead of me reading to myself.

Since then, the Holy Spirit speaks to my very soul when I am in His Word. Isaiah 41:10 has been my life verse, "Do not be afraid, for I am with you. Do not be afraid, for I am your God. I will strengthen you and help you. I will uphold you with my victorious right hand." I go to it often for help. God spoke to me on the couch during the early days of my marriage, when I believed in God and Rob did not. He spoke to my stewing mindset when anger was on the tip of my tongue. God spoke to me when I faced breast cancer. He speaks the most perfect words to uplift my insecure self. He even speaks through this verse as I grow a ministry called United in Love and in the writing of this book.

He is speaking to me while I grieve and wrestle with adjusting to parenting our adult children who I so loved raising. My favorite name is "Mama." Isaiah 41:10, along with many other verses, keeps me going. I am focused on God so that when Jesus comes for me one day, I will be ready for Him.

After walking with God for forty-plus years now, I can attest to the fact that God loves me, and He loves you. Whenever I go to Him, the pieces of my life fall into place. My path is always cleared for what He has for me, and He will do the same for you. I find this amazing and humbling since I cause myself so much distress when I doubt and throw fits; however, God waits patiently for me to look up. My flesh wrestles with the Holy Spirit. I always hear, "Look up, Carol. Trust me." And He is saying the same thing to you. He is welcoming you in His love.

In my relationship with God, I relinquish the control over to Him. I have peace as He:

- gives me clarity on the problems at hand, whether in relationships or tasks;
- lifts me up to the Rock, aka God, where He settles my tumultuous soul;
- redirects my priorities and helps me align what is important;
- gives me wisdom to live out His ways;
- has never once failed to follow through on what He tells me—never; and
- keeps His Word—and I want you to know, He won't fail you.

The safest and most secure place to be is in God's presence. You discover His presence when you read His very words. No matter what, God is with you. He knows what your needs are. He knows your passions, hopes and desires. Psalm 116:1-2 describes my relationship with God. "I love the LORD because He hears my voice and my prayer for mercy. Because He bends down to listen, I will pray as long as I have breath!"

God began good work within me. He had to place me in a foreign land with my unbelieving husband. He had to strip me of my comforts, which caused me to look up. While it was not fun to endure, looking back, God has amazed me with all the answered prayers—those I have shared with Him as well as unspoken ones that I didn't even realize my heart was asking. God hears my heart.

He is all I need, and it is my prayer that you discover that He is all you need.

Are you ready to fall in love? Are you ready to belong and know who you are?

Chapter One

WE NEED ONE ANOTHER

*"God decided in advance to adopt us into
His own family by bringing us to Himself through Jesus Christ.
This is what He wanted to do, and it gave Him great pleasure."*
— Ephesians 1:5

In the spring of 1975, I sat daydreaming at my school desk. Summer was approaching, and it couldn't come soon enough. I had to attend my brother's wedding first before enjoying my summer adventures. I was ten-years-old and in third grade, and this was my fourth family wedding. I already had a brother-in-law, and now I would have three sisters-in-law. When you are the youngest of eight and most of your siblings are adults, you have weddings to attend.

While I loved school and weddings, summer meant freedom from germy boys, spelling tests, and Mom and Dad. I was allowed to spend my summer months in Vermont with my two sisters. Kathy and I traveled from our home in Upper Michigan to our married sister Christine's home when school got out in June, and we returned in August before school resumed. I enjoyed many summers of carefree freedom, from the summer after kindergarten through high school.

I was able to have these summer havens because Mom and Dad taught us that after college, you go where the work takes you. This meant my oldest sister was going on an adventure with her new husband. I had been her flower girl, at age four, when Christine had gotten married, and a new job opportunity for Stan meant moving a thousand miles away.

This particular move was hard on Chris. She had been Mom's princess while growing up between five brothers who had found mischief wherever they went. She had dreamed of having a sister. Then one December, her dream came true when Kathy was born. Three Decembers later, I came along, and Chris was beyond elated to have not one but two sisters that she could dote on. But now she had to move far away. How were we going to be together?

God made a way, and my summer adventures in New England began. God is like that. He provides opportunities through which we can bond with each other. This pleases God. God wants to experience life with you.

"God grafts us into His family, and we receive the blessings that God has promised"
- Romans 11:17

My parents were older when Kathy and I came along, so our going out east gave my parents their own haven and some downtime. Chris was like a surrogate mother who tended to us and made sure we had swimming lessons, taught us how to ride bikes, and took us to the dentist. We would go camping, enjoy the rides at Riverside Amusement

Park, and take drives to the ocean. Chris and Stan treated us like their very own children. You could say we helped prepare them for their three children who came along eventually. It was like they adopted us as their own.

"Love Will Keep Us Together" by Captain and Tennille was the hit song in my third-grade year. This was a fitting song for us "kolme siskoa," which is Finnish for three sisters. We had already had three summers together, and God would provide many more. That song, along with ABBA's wonderful music, made for some fun bonding times wherever we went.

Love Takes on Various Faces

Love is the cord that connects people. None of us can deny that. It is around us like the air we breathe. It is an invisible glue that binds human beings together. Nothing truly matters except love. We see this when people face a loss of some kind. Things that divide us dissolve when saturated in love. A deep healing can take place. Even in horrendous circumstances like poverty, hunger, and racial injustice, God offers hope and a way out of trying circumstances. We see this hope in organizations that bring relief to hard-hit areas.

Love that is offered to another person is the most precious sight to see. Think of a mother seeing her child right after birth. It truly is love at first sight. She is so enamored by this little life that grew within her womb. When two people meet for the first time, something transformative happens. It is a bond that binds, like the love between sisters or a couple that is ready to say, "I do."

Those who can't bear children can experience this deepened bond as well. De-

This is the essence of God. His love unites us and bonds us together.

spite the heartache that infertility brings, love can be offered through adoption. They become a family that is built on relationships coming together, in which love remains at the core. This is the epitome of the relationship that God wants with us.

I have seen this happen in my family. After losing their youngest daughter, who was born with a major health issue, my brother and sister-in-law considered adoption. They chose to adopt a little girl from Korea. Kimberley became a part of the family as an infant. Mary's heart melted when she saw her daughter for the first time. It was love at first sight. Mary recalled, "I didn't know a heart could hold so much love for a child [not born of your body]. I was her mommy and I loved her."

Now stop and imagine the love that God has for you, which *began before you were even conceived*. Ephesians 1:4 speaks of this, "Even before He made the world, God loved us and chose us in Christ to be holy and without fault in His eyes." God had you in mind when He created the world.

On my husband's side of the family, his sister and her husband had wanted children, but after multiple miscarriages, they chose adoption, and twice took trips to Romania to bring home a daughter and then a son. Their daughter had been left at an orphanage at two months old on Christmas Eve. From that time to when Vic and Maria took her, Angela had never seen the outside. She cried a lot. Everything was new. But when love becomes the center, one promptly adapts to one's surroundings. Angela adapted quickly. Angela was the name given to her by her biological mother. It means "Messenger of God," so Vic and Maria thought it was fitting for the years of barrenness they had experienced.

The second trip to Romania was a bit easier. Vic stayed home with Angela, so Yvonne, Maria's mother, went with her. I remember my mother-in-law telling me that it was like watching Maria give birth. "To see her face when Devon was placed in her arms was priceless." He, too, adapted quickly.

I want you to begin to understand that you are a gift that God created. No matter the circumstances around your birth, He has always loved you. You are not an accident. In Ephesians 1, you read how we all bring God pleasure and joy when we choose to follow His Son. Take a few minutes and read this passage to see for yourself. Begin to believe that you are here for a very special purpose.

I have a friend who pursued adoption. Kris was both excited and apprehensive when she got the call that a little girl had been chosen for her in China. She had learned to trust God in the waiting and wondering. The agency sent her pictures of Kayla at four months old. "She was the most beautiful child I ever laid eyes on," Kris remembered. Kris and her mother arrived in China along with eight couples who were making their forever families.

Kayla, only eight-months-old, placed her hand in her mama's hair and put her head on her shoulder, as if to say, "I'm home." Praises to God were in Kris's heart for all He had done along the journey. She cried, "How God made me ready for this moment!" *The love of God can never be broken.* There is nothing in this world that can sever it.

After being barren for ten-plus years, my niece gave birth to a little boy. He is the youngest of three. You see, Britney and her husband, Paul, had adopted two children, one Black and one White, before their third child arrived. The beauty of God rang true as they became a family of five.

The blending of different backgrounds is what makes up the family unit, and it is a beautiful thing. Each fits perfectly with one another, bringing joy and happiness. Ethnicity, health issues, backgrounds, and any other differences *do not stop love.* His love is unending and without borders. It is a bonding agent that helps with adapting to your surroundings and is a force that cannot be quenched.

Love Is Committed Service

As you continue to read this book, you will come to realize the cost that it took for God to redeem man. You will see how God is with us for the long haul. He has been with His creation since Adam and Eve walked on this earth. He faithfully sees us through this life until He takes us from it. There has never been a moment in your life in which God has not been with you, ever.

I have seen how the process to adopt a child is extensive and exhausting, not to mention expensive. It takes a commitment on your part to want to go the long haul to bring home another life. You will not know what the future holds. You may not know anything about the child's family history, including any medical issues. You simply go on the desire to love. It is a risk you are willing to take. It's a risk that you find to be well worth it despite the hard work that is involved in raising another life.

Every person of any ethnicity has a place to call home when they belong to God.

Whether through adoption or biological pregnancies, loving another life is the epitome of human relationships. We need each other. God fashioned us this way so that we learn what love is by interacting with one another.

Marriage is a facet of love in which we rely on one another and share life together. It is a commitment to another person despite not knowing what tomorrow will be. It's a life-long process of discovering new things each day and learning how to coexist. I have been blessed to see commitment in my family. My parents were married for forty-six years, and my in-laws made it to fifty-five years. All my siblings and I are married to our first spouses, except for one of my brothers. His wife passed away from cancer, and he has since remarried. Many

"God's mercies are new every morning"
- Lamentations 3:23

nieces and nephews have gotten married and they, too, are experiencing lasting marriages. It is quite something in this day and age of broken promises.

I have read about a sixty-five-year marriage. That is many years of service. The key to this couple's marriage was that they fixed issues in their relationship instead of throwing it out. It's not about getting your way or how happy or unhappy you are. It's about trust, security, and being there for the other person. Marriage is like a foundation, one which can weather the ups and downs of life. *We all seek safety and security, and servant-style love accomplishes this.* Jesus Christ came to show us what this style of love looks like and how to live it out daily.

Love Is Consistent

Do you have memories of strong foundations within your family? If you don't, I have great news. Even in the midst of a cracked relationship, love heals. If your memories are soured by hardships and brokenness, be encouraged that His love not only picks up the pieces but restores them back to wholeness, and you can begin again.

Homes are built upon strong marital foundations. Not perfect homes, but intact ones. Love heals imperfections. I look back and think about my relatives' homes and how they never changed décor. Each time I visited, the sights and smells were familiar and homey. I knew that I belonged. This is heartwarming and gives stability to one's life.

Along with many siblings, I also have a slew of aunts and uncles. My mom was the youngest of eleven, and my dad had four siblings. I had two elderly aunts, Alma and Elsie, who lived together. They would always have pink candy mints, and they never seemed to mind

God wants you to get familiar with Him. He will become home to you.

that I ate my fair share when I visited. Then there was my Auntie Sylvie with her bright red hair. She had a red table in the nook of her kitchen where we would sit eating cookies. Such simple things that became a part of who I am. These simple interactions build upon themselves to become one's legacy. As we deepen our faith in God, He builds up our lives to the point that we become at home in His presence. God wants to be in a relationship with you.

Years ago, homes remained in the era that they were established. Certain smells or sights bring back memories of one's past. This gives the feeling of security—something you can count on—and this consistency establishes deep roots that can weather the storms in life. I find it troubling that we are losing the traditions of our pasts. We gain so much from those who have gone before us. Each generation teaching the next one.

Past Christmases have been fond memories for me. My parents loved the holidays. Starting with Thanksgiving at my brother's house in Wisconsin, family would gather for the holiday weekend. My dad and brothers would deer hunt, and my sisters and I—along with our nieces and nephews—would shop on Black Friday after cooking and eating the day before. There would always be a skit created by my sisters to entertain the boys after deer hunting. *With many memories and laughter, roots of love were made.*

After returning from Wisconsin, my mom would pull out all the Christmas decorations, and we would decorate the house for Christmas. Christmas music would be playing while we hung ornaments on the tree and put up the holiday village of glittery little cardboard houses, the ceramic green tree with colored bulbs, and the giant plastic candles that lit up the front porch. The 1970s had great decorations.

Mom baked so many treats that she could have opened her own bakery. Every year, Mom would make Dad his favorite cookie: prune tarts. She exhibited true love because they weren't the easiest to prepare, but she made them anyway. She faithfully grumbled each December. My home smelled the best, looked the coziest, and was the most welcoming to family and friends during this festive time.

Now, as I travel back to Upper Michigan, so many memories come to mind of where I grew up: Christmases past, seeing familiar scenery like Lake Superior in the distance or pasty shops in every town. Make the short "a" sound, please, when you say *pasty*. Think of a calzone, only better. Instead of pizza toppings inside a pastry crust, you have either beef or pork mixed with potatoes, carrots, and onions.

I have fond memories of my past that help me to continue to build upon it with my own children—and one day with grandchildren.

The Price Being Paid for Shallow Love

Unfortunately, today we seem to be lacking the very things that I mentioned above. One's heritage seems to have become insignificant. Today it is about what is new, exciting, and fresh. Tomorrow it will be something else, and we are allowing our lives to be dictated by short-lived fads. We live in the present moment, *as if tomorrow is guaranteed*. Perhaps a pandemic is a blessing in disguise. God is bringing us back to simple things so that we can deepen the roots of love. This generation, as well as future ones, are in dire need of it.

There is no sense of intimacy within the family unit, and with all the social media and filled calendars, fellowship is left at the doorstep. No wonder marriages and other relationships get strained so easily. We are not living with the intentions that will build the essential foundation for meaningful relationships. Life has become individualistic, and we can see the results, like broken marriages and children living with many sets of rules. What I mean is that some children have to adjust to Mom's rules at her house, Dad's rules at his house, daycare's rules, school rules, etc. *Life becomes about survival more than love.*

I believe people do not want to live this way. Although we struggle with balancing it all, *how do we stop the madness of this shallow style of living?* Is it possible to live in a manner in which you can flourish and those you love can flourish? There is an answer to that, and it is Yes! We each possess a key that unlocks the wonders of the world. If you used your key, you would discover a great treasure that would change your world into a world worth living in.

Society has become a race of selfish fulfillments and entertainment. Man's mindset is all about *now*. Yesterday is gone and tomorrow is not here. Legacies are not being cherished and upheld. Marriages and families aren't surviving with this kind of mentality. *Love is being diluted instead of being the driving force.*

Love Is Worth Fighting For

Our marriage is not exempt from the onslaught of diluted love. Rob and I have to battle our relationship daily. It's a fight to discern what is important and what is trivial. We had to learn to fight in a productive way and communicate more effectively so that we could understand each other better. We came together with different kinds of baggage that got dumped out on the floor of marital bliss, and we soon found it was not blissful! Suitcases of *me, myself*, and *I* were the heaviest bags that we carried into our early married years.

Rob and I are thankful that we allowed God to change and subdue the messy traits that we each brought into our relationship. We were fresh out of college, full of ourselves, with hopes and dreams, and a desire to be together. We quickly found that marriage brought out my stubbornness, anger, and perfectionism, while Rob dealt with his bullheadedness and his pride. We were the captains of our own ships, and soon realized that life wasn't about *me, myself*, and *I* anymore.

Both of us struggled at learning to share life with one another. It didn't help us any that we were the youngest of our families nor that we both came from homes with an angry parent who had expressed themselves verbally. Many disputes have been warred in our thirty-plus years. However, when we were both willing to change, grow, and mature, something beautiful happened. God has taught us to love correctly—more importantly, how to love unconditionally like He does.

We realized that marriage becomes long-lasting when each spouse determines to be what the other needs. Rob and I have had years of learning this kind of love. It is not easy. It is humbling and tiring at times, but it is a choice that is so worth it.

Love is a commitment that resembles a covenant and not a contract. God makes a covenant with His children. We see this throughout scripture. Look at Jeremiah 31:33: "But this is the new covenant I will make with the people of Israel after those days, declares the LORD: I will put my instructions deep within them, and I will write them on their hearts. I will be their God, and they will be my people."

God will choose you every time. You are that important to Him.

In the following chapters, you will see how first *I learned to live committed to God*, which then trickled down to loving my husband, kids, and everyone else. I will go into more detail about the struggles that Rob and I faced. What I hope and pray for is that you will see how God revealed Himself to me in the midst of my messy, broken ways. I did not have to get my act together first. He embraced me and taught me how to love myself, which I might add is a work in progress until He takes me home. From there, He taught me how to love Rob.

Love in Everyday Life

Love is a lifestyle in which commitment plays an important component. We see it in the family unit with marriage and new families. It is also in everyday life like eating healthy, paying bills, showing up for work, keeping promises to others—the list is endless. Commitment is a glue that holds relationships together, just like love. We can depend on each other.

Siblings carry a special commitment of love. I should know, I have a bunch of them, and they are priceless to me. You share life with them and experience the same things while growing up. I had a front row seat to watching commitment lived out with my six older siblings. I learned that it is messy, hard work, though enriching at the same time. As a youngster, I saw that receiving an education is important, what various marriages looked like beyond my parents' marriage, and that raising children is not for sissies when I became an aunt at the age of three. I grew up with a good understanding of how life should be lived by watching my family.

Kathy and I were the caboose of our family's train and grew up sharing our lives. Life lessons are learned when you share a bedroom. We fought like cats and dogs, but we were each other's warriors. *The experiences we all go through prepare us to find God.* He purposely places us in certain settings so we will come to see our need for a savior.

God found me amidst anger, debilitating shyness, and fragile insecurity, and, at the same time, as someone who was kind-hearted, creative, and spoiled by those around me. I want you to know that God met me and helped me. He will do the same for you, no matter what your traits may be. God fashioned each of us in a unique way.

Pets are another example of love and commitment. They were the best training for me before we had children. I was very obsessive about cleanliness, and everything had its place. Anything out of place caused irritation within me. Pets helped me to calm down and be okay with dirt and hair. Rob and I have had two yellow labs that taught me much and brought us joy. We got them as puppies, and together Bo and Daisy gave us twenty-four years of happiness, plus a truckload of dog hair. I soon learned that sweeping was useless, and the vacuum cleaner became my best friend.

Four years ago, we took in a rescue dog. Lola needed to experience love and commitment. At a year old, she had come from an abusive environment in Alabama. Animal Rescue removed her and brought her to Minnesota. She arrived timid and scared. Her foster dad began the process of tending to her gently and lovingly for one month, and then we adopted her.

By giving her gentleness, patience, and room to grow, she has learned to trust us. She is happy and free; she loves her walks and has learned how to play. She is now more comfortable around people and loves to play with other dogs. She simply needed a safe place where love and patience would follow her from that moment on. By our side, she knows she is safe. *When one receives the proper care, one blooms as one is intended to and brings joy to others.* And this is how God treats us when we follow Him. He loves us so that we can bloom and share ourselves with others. He redeems the wrongs in our life and remolds us with all good things that matter to Him. He adopts us and forever more we have unconditional and committed love from our Father.

The safest place to be is in the arms of God.

The armed services exemplify love and commitment on a grand scale. One is willing to fight and die so that his brother or sister from another mother can be free. This should stop us in our tracks. This good life that many of us experience in the United States is because of the countless men and women who have fought to keep this country free. Thankfulness should be spewing from our hearts as we nurture our brave heroes.

My father-in-law served twenty-six years in the air force, and my brother and a nephew each served. Most of us have uncles or grandfathers who have served. They truly exhibit respect, integrity, and faithfulness. We see a noble legacy from which to learn from. *Those who serve others understand what truly matters in life. They understand the value of life, love, commitment, and teamwork.*

We need to live out these values if we want to see unity among ourselves. We are of one body: the body of Christ.

I want to share a story of God's style of love and commitment. It happened between friends many, many years ago, in a village called Capernaum. A group of men wanted to help heal a paralyzed man. In their day, medicine and cures were in short supply. These friends heard of a man who could heal paralysis and many other diseases. So, they took it upon themselves to make sure that the paralyzed man would get the help he needed.

They were committed to getting their friend help. They approached the house where this miracle worker was staying. They found it quite crowded with no room for anyone else to enter. Everyone had heard about this man who healed and performed miracles, but that didn't stop these four friends. They went up on the roof and cut a hole, then they lowered the man down right in front of Jesus, and *he was healed.*

You can find this story in Mark 2:1-12 in the Bible. No barrier can stop you from discovering God's love. *All we need to be is willing.*

What If Love Wasn't Available?

Many people come from homes where commitment was thrown to the side, and everyone lived in survival mode. In such homes, all they have seen is brokenness. I want you to know that healing and restoration are within reach, at a place where you can begin building treasured memories. Hope is available. All you need is tender loving care from God, the Lover of your soul.

Whatever degree of love you have experienced, there is a treasured love that lies within you that can bloom and grow into a fullness that will radiate to those around you. I may have come from a safe home but not a perfect one. I may have had my physical needs met, but I struggled mentally, emotionally, and spiritually—and I still do. We all struggle in this world that is marred and imperfect. No one comes from a perfect home.

We have seen how man is committed to one another. Maybe we are not perfectly committed, but we do care about those around us. We need one another. Our society seems to have lost its way. However, with a new mindset, it can be turned around. We can become a people mighty and strong. By simply adding love and commitment to someone's life, beauty and purpose flourish.

I have seen it by watching my adopted nieces and nephew, who started out underdeveloped when they arrived at their new homes, but with love and care, they flourished exponentially. It was amazing to see how fast they grew. I have watched my rescue dog, Lola, learn to trust, and as she did, she flourished. It has been fun to watch her personality develop.

God wants us to trust Him. Amazing things happen when we do.

I want you to know that God is the Lover of your soul! Despite how your life began, what choices you have made, or where you are right now, you are loved so perfectly and completely by your Heavenly Father. You were loved by Him before you were born as He was creating you in your mother's womb and right from the first breath you took. Psalm 22:9-10 says, "You brought me safely from my mother's womb and led me to trust you at my mother's breast. I was thrust into your arms at my birth. You have been my God from the moment I was born." Stop for a moment and drink in that truth.

God's love is an unconditional relationship, one that is worth seeking, and one that you are drawn to. He gave man an everlasting covenant after flooding the earth due to man's wickedness. He gives you a rainbow after a rainstorm when the sun comes back out to brighten the sky. The rainbow represents that God will never flood the earth again to destroy all life. He has held true to this promise. Every time you see a rainbow, it is a visible sign from God that He sees you. The rainbow is a reminder that you can trust God to lead your life. He keeps His promises! You can learn about this in Genesis 6-9.

As you learn and come to understand God's commitment, you will also learn how you are to live in response to Him. In Psalm 148, praise is reiterated thirteen times towards God. The heavens praise Him and the earth praises Him and "He has made His people strong." What a reason to get to know the God that loves you.

You will be strong when your heart is praising Him. May you fall in love with God and His Son, as I have. May you find His Truth within your own heart and let God reveal Himself to you. Let's keep discovering true love. Your marriage, family, community, and country will all flourish because of you. Your world will change in a way that is positive and uplifting. I need you to be who God called you to be. You need me to be living out His calling. We need each other.

Chapter two

LOVE COMES IN A PACKAGE

"May the grace of the Lord Jesus Christ,
the love of God, and the fellowship of the
Holy Spirit be with you all."
— 2 Corinthians 13:14

What comes to mind when you think of something that comes in a set of three? I know, you are thinking of we three sisters. My sisters and I have that kind of impact on everyone. No one is the same after being around us, let me tell you. While I'm laughing over this, anyone that knows us would agree to this fact—and please don't ask our brothers what they think. What do they know? When our five sisters-in-law are included, we do have a grand time together.

Where there are three of something, we usually find harmony and strength, unless they are siblings. Take a cord for example. According to the Merriam-Webster's dictionary, a cord is made of flexible material consisting of several strands that are woven together. A cord of three things or people cannot be broken, and it becomes quite strong. Ecclesiastes 4:9-12 gives a great example of this. "Two people are better off than one, for they can help each other succeed. If one person falls, the other can reach out and help. But someone who falls alone is in real trouble. Likewise, two people lying close together can keep each other warm. But how can one be warm alone? A person standing alone can be attacked and defeated, but two can stand back-to-back and conquer. Three are even better, for a triple-braided cord is not easily broken."

Let's look at some other examples in our world that have three components. I can think of several examples that are simple and that we interact with every day, like color. It is my favorite. I love art. There is a picture of me as a toddler coloring on the wall. God started molding me at an early age. This resulted in my obtaining a bachelor of fine arts degree in graphic design.

Throughout my childhood, I would sit and make paper dolls for hours. I still could. Put a craft in front of me, and you won't see me for the rest of the day. I would get so excited when my kids had to do school projects and I was allowed to help. With my art prowess and their dad's engineering skillset, the kids looked really good handing in their assignments. Picture me beaming from ear to ear.

Anyhow, color is special, and it takes only three colors to make up the whole spectrum of hues. Our world is so colorful and vibrant. Three colors can create a Crayola tower of 150 hues or more. I love how three simple colors can outfit the world around us, from the changing leaves in fall, to the fresh and pure whiteness of snow in winter, to blooming peonies and lilacs in spring and the lush greens of summer. Eyesight is truly a beautiful gift.

Another example is water. We use it every day and in so many ways. Water has one-part oxygen and two-parts hydrogen and it has three states: liquid, solid, and gas. We can boil it, freeze it, drink it, and even immerse ourselves in it. It also hydrates, cleans, and even makes electricity. We can see the beauty of water as in a lake or ocean, and we can feel water as it is falling down from the sky to refresh us on a hot day. God covered two-thirds of the earth with it, and our bodies are made up mostly of water. We need it for survival, and it is essential for life, just like love and commitment are essential. God is faithful to give us what we need.

Bask in the beauty around you. God is saying hello to you.

Think about your ears. They contain three small bones that, when they work together, create a symphony of different sounds, like that of a baby crying when he is first born, or the snoring of your pet sleeping at the foot of the bed, or a clap of thunder when a rainstorm is approaching. How about the bell going off and students scrambling out of their seats, knowing that it is the end of their school day or that summer vacation has begun? The myriad sounds in our world are incalculable, and they add depth to life.

When three parts operate in harmony as one, something beautiful takes place. Look at faith, hope, and love: a universal triad that is recognized globally. These three attributes originate from our Creator and are like building blocks for the human race. You can see by these examples that when things work in unison, life has depth and meaning.

The True Trio

I know of another trio that works in harmony with each other like the ones you've read about. They have always existed and are of absolute perfection. Time and space do not limit them. You would use words like *honesty,*

God does not want you to miss out on what He has for you.

integrity, faithful, creative, unconditional, and *the origin-of-life* to describe them. Whenever you refer to them, they deserve their titles to be capitalized. Prestigious, dignified, and honorable are a few more ways to describe them. *Human languages cannot fully describe them.*

This trio is three unique persons, yet each can act as one. Our simple minds will not be able to fully understand how God the Father, God the Son, and God the Holy Spirit are three in one. It is one of life's mysteries. It would be impossible for God to reveal everything about life and Himself to us. Our minds could not hold it in. He is simply too vast. The notion that He simply exists and has no beginning or end—it is unfathomable to our human minds. John 1:1-5 says, "In the beginning, the Word already existed. The Word was with God and the Word was God. He existed in the beginning with God. God created everything through Christ and nothing was created except through His Son. The Word, being Jesus, gave life to everything that was created, and His life brought light to everyone. The light shines in the darkness, and the darkness can never extinguish it."

God gives of Himself in three amazing ways so that you can come to know Him personally, in a way that you can comprehend who He is.

Consider the Source

Before we look at each person of the Trinity, let's consider the source from which you will come to understand who they are. Think of your best friend. You know him really well, and you trust him. Therefore, when he gives you advice, you listen—most of the time. While there are many sources to gain information from, they may not be the most reliable. You are going to discover how the Trinity is the source of all truth. You can be rest assured that you are in the right place when you go to God.

Today, you have instant access to everything. It is like instant knowledge at your fingertips. Little time and effort are required to find information about anything. You are accustomed to quick access on any subject. While technology makes life easier, it isn't always the best. The issue now is with accuracy from the source. Fake news has become a real thing. There is not a true plumb line for accuracy and authenticity. A plumb line is used by builders to make sure the structure is erected perfectly true. In the book of Amos, God shows Amos a plumb line to see if a wall is straight (Amos 7:7-8).

Many topics are trivial and don't warrant a high score on what I call the *truth-meter*. Examples would be looking up recipes or learning how to knit. I have learned how to knit, and I found videos and instructions on the web to be very helpful. My daughter became lactose intolerant and gluten free, and finding recipes that do not have milk or gluten in them has been simple. My husband became interested in building a cabin—no problem finding out how to do that. For my son's birthday, he messages me links for gift ideas. In many ways, you can find an array of sources that will give you answers related to your interests and hobbies. You don't need to worry about whether something is true or not with topics like these.

But what about the not-so-trivial things in life? The issues of life that affect our neighborhoods, towns, cities, country, and society as a whole. The constitution and civil laws are being undermined. Right and wrong are continually being challenged while people are wanting to change or erase history. Foundational certainties are being replaced with new and exciting ideas.

There is a growing lack of respect for authority, like police officers, elected officials and school teachers, to name a few. Our freedom of speech is abused and the value of life has depreciated, and we wonder *why hatred and violence are running amok.*

Even with science and medicine confirming when life begins, there is such divisiveness over it. Right and wrong are not what is important. It's about each of us being seen and heard in our own way. There is no more unity, and society is revealing the ill-effects of it. Chaos ensues instead of us coming together to work out issues that arise.

Disarray happens when we turn our backs on God.

Look at what our society deems important, like reality TV. People are willing to get naked with a stranger, lay in a bed of snakes to face a fear, exploit themselves in hopes of gaining a marriage proposal, or simply exploit themselves for fame or fortune. The pursuit of the American dream has become more than owning a home with a white picket fence. It is now about the luxury estate filled with big-boy toys. Young families are eating up this materialistic lifestyle. *We have become desensitized and numb to what truly has value.*

When it comes to issues that affect our lives and our society, we need to seek a source that will provide stability, peace, and productivity—a source that can teach how to live properly so that everyone benefits. As many educated scholars have studied mankind and the world that we live in, one has to wonder whose viewpoint is right? Everyone wants to be right and to be seen, which has turned into a shallow way of life and a shallow love.

A Reliable Source

Despite the ways of man, God has given a reliable source to follow and learn from. He has been leading man since the beginning of our existence on this earth. It started in the Garden of Eden where God walked with Adam and Eve. Genesis 3:8 says, "When the cool evening breezes were blowing, the man and his wife heard the LORD God walking about in the garden." This is a personal God, who after creating man and woman, remained in their midst, talked to, and guided them.

This is true today. God walks with you and me. You can find out how and why He does it by reading the Bible. The first four books of the New Testament are called the Gospels: Matthew, Mark, Luke, and John. This is a great place to begin learning how God wants you to know the love that He has for you. Throughout the pages, you will learn about the history of man and his behavior. You will come to realize that man is no different today than he was back when Adam and Eve lived on earth, and how God is the same yesterday, today, and forever.[1] This makes Him relatable and reliable.

Learning how the Bible came together aroused a thirst in me to read it. Forty authors from various backgrounds were inspired by God to write down things that remain authentic through today. The Bible is ageless. These forty authors wrote over a span of 1,500 years. They did not know each other, but they shared with each other what they were writing down. There is no other book like it.

These writings have been confirmed by historians and archaeologists throughout the centuries. Take note as you read through scripture that you can cross-reference identical verses from various authors speaking of the same thing without knowing each other. The Bible is one of the top best-selling books ever. That is reason enough to check it out.

Many men who have tried to disprove the authenticity of the Bible can't find any errors. Think about that, finding no errors in a book written by many authors over that span of time. It would be impossible to replicate without God intervening and speaking to us.

Have you ever played the children's game called "Telephone Operator"? You sit in a circle and a person whispers a phrase in the ear of the person next to them. Each person whispers what they heard to the next person and so on. Then the last person says out loud what the first person said. You know what happens. It is never the same. So, how in the world were the authors of the Bible so clear and accurate?

Perfect Love

Let's transition to a cozy setting and meet the Lover(s) of your soul. I'm going to pick my absolute favorite: Christmas morning. Picture yourself there. The tree is lit, the fire is going in the fireplace, coffee is brewing, cinnamon rolls are baking in the oven, and presents are waiting to be opened under the tree. It's been snowing all night and it is still coming down. It is perfect, Lord, thank you.

You notice an exceptionally beautiful present tucked under the tree, wrapped in gold, shimmery paper with a red satin ribbon tied around it. The heart-shaped tag has your name on it. You are intrigued. You untie the ribbon and open the box. Inside, you find three more boxes wrapped in gold, each with a tag that says, "You are loved perfectly."

The first box is from the Triune God, God the Father. He shares who He is with you. He is your Creator. He made you with tender, loving care. He is the God of purpose and order, which means that your birth is not random or accidental. You are here with purpose. Even if your beginning was not a pretty picture, full of hurt and loneliness, your life at this time in history is vital and unique to His will and calling.

I wrestle with God about why He loves me. I have many questions about why He made me the way He did. One thing I hate about myself is how insecure I am in my thinking. I feel like I make life hard for myself. Every day, it is a battle to keep thinking positive. I seem to naturally navigate towards negativity. I question why I was so painfully shy and scared in my early years.

God's love is a redeeming love.

I am happy to say that God has built me up. Once, I was an introvert who didn't like people; now I am the opposite. While I am still timid over new things, I let myself experience unfamiliar things. I am willing to try. As a child, fear halted me, so much so that it fed my stubbornness. I am proud to say that bravery has birthed another love within me: roller coasters. I love the thrill of them. I feel so confident and strong after getting off.

God is not thwarted by the woes of man. God is not scared off by bad choices. God doesn't rescind Himself from you because you are flawed. He is bigger and can overcome what man dishes out. He remains committed to you. There is never a moment in which God is not loving you.

My friend Tiffany was abandoned by her mother and pretty much by her father. She was the product of an affair. Throughout her childhood and teen years, she was mistreated and tossed aside, and she felt abandoned and unloved. Her dark past followed her into her adult years where she lived a turbulent lifestyle. *But God saw and He pursued.* Today, she is in the process of healing and becoming whole. She now has a Father that is there for her and loves her wholly.

That is the business of God your Father. He sees. He heals. As part of her healing therapy, Tiffany would draw pictures of her early years. In every picture, a bearded man was crying. I asked her who he was, and why he was in every picture. She said, "That is Jesus. He saw everything happening to me. He has always been there with me."

Tiffany has experienced God's redeeming love. She allowed God to get close to her, and she responded back to the love He was offering her. He is the Lover of her soul, forever. She takes the love that God offers her and spills it out onto others. Her soul is alive because of Him, and I have seen *God heal her from the inside out.*

No one has a say in their birth. No one has a say in who their parents are. God has a purpose for why I am my parents' youngest child. You don't have a say in what you look like, what personality traits you will carry, or what your strengths or weaknesses are. You do not have a say in whether you are born into money or poverty. Nothing. We all come into this world the same way, and we all will leave this earth at some point. Birth and Death. We all have this in common.

What makes our birth-and-death stories hard are questions like the following, which nag at us:

- Why are some people born on easy street and some born into adversity?
- Why are some more gifted than others?
- Why are some born into loving environments and some in abusive ones?
- Why are some better looking than others?
- Why do people have to struggle with birth defects?
- Why do some receive blessings easily and others have to struggle for each thing?

It seems unfair, and we blame God for this unfairness and injustice. In the following chapters, you will learn why *there is this unfairness, and it isn't God's fault.*

The Vastness of God

In Genesis 1, you can see how God the Father created the heavens and the earth. Read about the galaxy, and be amazed at His hand in creating space, planets, and stars. Google the size of the universe and see if you can comprehend its vastness.

Now, think about yourself and how you fit into such vastness. While you will feel very insignificant, God says that you are not. Psalm 8:3-6 says, "When I look at the night sky and see the work of your fingers, the moon and the stars you set in place, what are mere mortals that you should think about them, human beings that you should care for them? You made them only a little lower than God and crowned them with glory and honor. You gave them charge of everything you made, putting all things under their authority." Did you read how you are crowned with glory and honor? God takes your feelings of inadequacy and fills you with worthiness and purpose.

God the Father is present today. He is right in this very moment with you. He refers to Himself in scripture as the Great "I Am." At this very moment that you are taking a breath, He is loving you. He does not remain in the past nor does He wait for you in the future. He is with you today.

This is comforting as I write this book. The world is under quarantine from a very contagious virus. The hope for the world is a living God. The cure, God Himself.

God called Moses on a mission, one for which Moses did not feel qualified. To help with his doubts and fears, God used a burning bush to show Moses who He was. Read Exodus 3:1-15 and learn for yourself. God spoke to Moses and gave him the words that he would need to speak to aid in leading His people out of slavery from Egypt.

Egypt represents the bondage you are living in on this earth. He wants to free you from it. "God replied to Moses, 'I AM WHO I AM. Say this to the people of Israel: I AM has sent me to you.' God also said to Moses, 'Say this to the people of Israel: Yahweh, the God of your ancestors, the God of Abraham, the God of Isaac, and the God of

Jacob has sent me to you. This is my eternal name, my name to remember for all generations.'"[2]

Recently, I had a encounter with God similar to the one He had with Moses. Rob started a fire in the stove at our cabin where we were staying for the weekend. The air was cool that Sunday morning. I snuggled in my sleeping bag and opened my Bible and journal. As I studied the fire, rays of red light extended towards me, and the fire grew bigger. This is the only way to describe what I saw. I blinked several times and rubbed my eyes to clear my sight. The rays remained for several minutes.

God didn't speak audibly to me like He did to Moses, but He did place it in my heart that He is with me and He sees me. He wanted me to know that He was going to lead me forward. God is faithful to meet us where we are at, and He does it at the most impeccable times. I hope you see that God is perfect that way.

He is committed to me like He was to Moses, and He is committed to you. I came to believe God forty years ago, and He has never left me. His pursuing nature toward me has never ceased. I have stopped pursuing Him at times, but He has never stopped pursuing me. I have made some dumb decisions, but He has never turned His back on me. He sees the potential in me and what I can be, and He sees you. He sees you and I full of hope, purpose, and abundant love. God placed great potential within you.

God the Father is love. This is who He is. He is the Creator of love. He wanted to share love so He created man and woman, Adam and Eve. This makes us their descendants. God gave Adam and Eve a place to live and thrive where He and His children could enjoy one another.

But just three chapters into Genesis, an infraction occurred. Sin entered the picture. Despite this infraction, God remained who He is. He was and is committed. He had to make a hard choice about what to do with His defiant creation. He had to separate them from Himself. Adam and Eve had to leave the place where God resided and toil through life with free will on their back. *Love is like that, it gives room for expression, even if it grieves the Creator.* You will study the infraction more deeply in the next chapter to get a better understanding.

God is the very essence of love, and this makes love of great value. He created you in His own likeness. Genesis 1:27 says, "So God created human beings in His own image. In the image of God, He created them; male and female, He created them." If God is love and you are made in His image, then you are of love, too. This is how you are to act, offering it to others.

As you learned in chapter 1, love is the invisible glue that bonds you. Love is at the core of who you are. It was placed within you when you were growing in your mother's womb, and it remains as long as you live. Love will keep us together, and wherever love is offered, there is God.

The Gift of Your Forever Companion

It is time to come back to that Christmas morning, where you sit with a cinnamon roll in your hand. You open the second box and you learn about another person of the Trinity, the Holy Ghost or Spirit. He is your best friend. He is your Counselor, Comforter, and Companion. With Him, you are never alone. I repeat, *you are never alone.* I still need to be reminded of this often. Loneliness can have such

Knowing God is present with me right at this moment has been a strong building block to my foundation of faith.

a hold on me. I believe we all struggle with this emptiness, even as believers.

He is always willing to listen and mediate on your behalf with God the Father. Romans 8:26-27 says, "And the Holy Spirit helps us in our weakness. For example, we don't know what God wants us to pray for. But the Holy Spirit prays for us with groaning that cannot be expressed in words. And the Father who knows all hearts knows what the Spirit is saying, for the Spirit pleads for us believers in harmony with God's own will." The Holy Spirit will bring you to pertinent scriptures that will feed your thirsty soul.

He aids in answering prayers. Even before you ask, God is working on your behalf. When you look up, you will be astounded by all the perfectly planned coincidences. My friend, that is God wooing you *so that you will know with confidence that He is who He says He is.* He never leaves your side for He is committed to you and your well-being.

God the Spirit was the one who inspired ordinary men, the authors of the Bible, to write down the words of God so that you could read and learn today. It must have been puzzling, to say the least, when they wrote down what the Holy Spirit spurred into them. I am quite sure that even though it didn't make sense, they followed their hearts anyway. God wants you to follow His lead, even when you don't fully understand what He is doing.

Apostles and prophets found their lives becoming quite adventurous, fulfilling, tumultuous, upside down, and completely satisfying as they penned God's words and lived out His ways. They had what their hearts needed, *and this need is the same today for you.* God wants to awaken you. He wants you to run wild into the future secured by God.

The Spirit resides in a regenerated heart. The next few chapters will cover how your heart needs to be regenerated and set free. 2 Corinthians 3:17 says, "For the Lord is the Spirit and wherever the Spirit of the Lord is, there is freedom." This freedom cannot be found on this earth. This earth is bound in time and space, and your body is bound by these dimensions. However, God created you with an attribute that sets you apart from all living things—you have an ageless soul. I am fifty-four years old, which means my physical body is aging, but inside, *my spirit is young and alive.* I feel like I am the same age as my daughter who is twenty-three.

The final person of the Trinity is so amazing that He needs His own chapter. You will read about Jesus in chapter 3. The Old Testament prophesied about Him, and He is the reason that there is a New Testament. He brought love to this earth and extended freedom to man. He is Jesus Christ, God's very own Son. Because of Jesus, God's faithful love rained down on earth.

So, the next time your birthday rolls around or it is Christmas morning, and sitting before you is a gift, a present, a package from someone who loves you, remember this: God, the Holy Spirit, and His Son are wrapped up and waiting for you to open them so they can share their love with you. You are worth their love. You are worth their time they spend with you. You are worth it.

God says you are worthy of His love.

Here is the best part, you don't have to wait for a special day to receive their Gift of Love. You can open Him any day of the year. He is ready and waiting.

In the coming chapters, you will learn from scripture. Think of scripture as your compass that shows true north. It will always point you in the right direction so that you will be in the right place at the right time. *Pay attention to when God speaks more than once about something,* He wants you to grab hold of a truth and remember it. In Psalm 136, "His faithful love endures forever" is spoken twenty-six times in the twenty-six verses. Each verse tells of His commitment towards man, a commitment that is rooted in love. He will be faithful to you, I promise.

Chapter three

THE LOVE OF YOUR LIFE

"For God so loved the world
that He gave His one and only Son, so
that everyone who believes in Him will
not perish but have eternal life."
— John 3:16

Come back to that special Christmas morning. You are now opening the final gold-wrapped box. Your heart becomes flooded with warmth, and it starts pounding while your hands become sweaty. A shiver runs through your body as you realize that you are meeting the Lover of your soul. Tucked inside is a ring—not just any ring but a promise ring. Jesus promises to be with you forever. You put it on and it fits perfectly. God promises to love you forever, and He hopes that you will love Him back.

Remember in the last chapter when I mentioned an infraction that had occurred? Now, let's learn more about how this infraction messed things up. God created Adam and Eve and gave them a perfect garden to reside in. They could enjoy all things within the garden except for one tree. They were not to eat of the fruit from that particular tree or else death would come upon them.

Life was perfect in the garden: restful, beautiful, and relaxed. And Adam and Eve's needs were met. Then, they met Satan *who was up to no good*. He had a belligerent attitude, and he had the need to strike out. He greatly disliked harmony. The bond that he saw between God and man disgusted him. We first hear about him in Genesis 3 when he makes his debut. He was responsible for the infraction that was going to take place.

The Enemy Has a Past

This mischievous creature, our enemy, has a past that began before Genesis 1:1. Many don't realize it, but the Trinity and the angels had a life in heaven before the earth and man were created, and Satan was one of God's angels. His residence was that of perfect harmony. He had a job assignment that meant special privileges with God, *until the day that evil was found in him.*[1]

By reading Ezekiel 28:12-19, we discover his downfall from heaven down to earth. "You were a model of perfection, full of wisdom, and exquisite in beauty. You were in Eden, the Garden of God. Your clothing was adorned with very precious stone; red carnelian, pale-green peridot, white moonstone, blue-green beryl, onyx, green jasper, blue lapis lazuli, turquoise, and emerald. They were all beautifully crafted for you and set in the finest gold. They were given to you on the day you were created. I ordained and anointed you as the mighty angelic guardian. You had access to the holy mountain of God and walked among the stones of fire.

"You were blameless in all you did from the day you were created until the day evil was found in you. Your rich commerce led you to violence and you sinned. I banished you in disgrace from the mountain of God. I expelled you, O mighty guardian, from your place among the stones of fire. Your heart was filled with pride because of all your beauty. Your wisdom was corrupted by your love of splendor. I threw you to the ground and exposed you to the curious gaze of kings. You defiled your sanctuaries with your many sins and your dishonest trade. I brought fire out from within you, and it consumed you. I reduced you to ashes on the ground in the sight of all who were watching. All who knew you are appalled at your fate. You have come to a terrible end, and you will exist no more."

Satan had many sins and you can see how relatable they are to what we do. Satan tripped himself up with wealth, pride, the lure of appealing things, making deals dishonestly, taking shortcuts, and more. Do you also not struggle with these same things?

Isaiah 14:12-14 also describes what happened to him. "How you are fallen from heaven, O shining star, son of the morning! You have been thrown down to the earth, you who destroyed the nations of the world. For you said yourself, 'I will ascend to heaven and set my throne above God's stars. I will preside on the mountain of the gods far away in the north. I will climb to the highest heavens and be like the most High.'" That was his demise. He wanted God's job. He wanted to be God, so God had to remove him from His Presence.

Revelation 12:7-9 says, "Then there was war in heaven. Michael and his angels fought against the dragon and his angels. And the dragon lost the battle and he and his angels were forced out of heaven. This great dragon, the ancient serpent called the devil or Satan, the one deceiving the whole world, was thrown down to the earth with all his angels." Jesus even reported seeing for Himself that Satan fell from heaven like lightning.[2] And he has run amok in this world ever since, stirring up hatred and division wherever he goes.

This One Event Changed Everything

Do you notice a similarity between Satan and man? We want to be our own god. Let's keep reading and see how God handles such behavior. Back in the Garden where Satan lived, he lied, tricked, deceived, and twisted God's words around to suit his motives. Satan wanted to break the bond between God and man. In the Garden, Adam and Eve had every luxury under heaven, but they couldn't touch one tree, the tree of the knowledge of good and evil. So, what did Satan do? He went straight for Eve and danced with her emotions and intuitions. "Don't you want to be like God?" he suggested. Satan wanted to be like God, and he knew he could never be. So, he pulled down God's most precious creation, human beings.

It is tempting when one has a question dangling in front of her like the one Eve had. Who wouldn't want to be like God, to know all things and have great wisdom? Without batting an eye, she ate some of the fruit that God had told her not to. Then she turned to Adam, and he ate some. We will deal with Adam in the next chapter. But for right now, something dreadful had just happened, something irreparable, that deserved a change in course from God's original design.

God created man for Himself. He created a home that would satisfy all their needs. Life was good in the Garden. Humans could move freely about in paradise and enjoy any of their desires to the fullest. Referring to everything that He had created, God said it was good. Can you imagine what God felt with His creation? He was pleased, and it brought Him enjoyment.

Like I mentioned previously, love gives room for expression, and God wanted man to be able to be free and choose for himself, so He granted us free will. The serpent did not waste any time in ill-advising Eve. He knew that if he could get her to want something for herself, she would take the bait just as he had. Thousands of years later, we are no different.

How painfully difficult it must have been for God to usher out His beloved ones to a place that would cause a separation between

Him and His children. But as we know all too well, there are consequences for being disobedient. God banished Adam and Eve from the Garden.

While you may see this as rather harsh, God has to be who He is. He will always remain true to His character. As you walk closer and closer with God, you will become thankful for this attribute. He is committed to His creation. You see this throughout His Word.

God will always do what is best for His creation.

Life would no longer be simple for Adam, Eve, and their offspring. The serpent was cursed first. From that day forward, he would have to slither along the dirty ground. Eve was sentenced to painful childbearing, and Adam would rule over her. Genesis 3:14-19 speaks of the results of disobedience. Satan became a snake where he would crawl on his belly and grovel in the dust, and there would now be hostility between him and Eve. This is because a woman would give birth to God's Son later on in history. As for Adam, the ground was now cursed, and he would struggle to make a living amidst thorns and thistles. Life would now become a labor of love; God would give of Himself so that we would have a way of returning back to Him.

God Remains Committed

Despite the curse, God remains who He is. He is love. As time marches on, God remains committed and faithful to His people. He has never left man completely to himself. You see a bonded thread woven throughout history from Genesis to Revelation through which God faithfully leads His people. In Exodus 13:21, it says, "The LORD went ahead of them. He guided them during the day with a pillar of cloud, and He provided light at night with a pillar of fire. He allowed them to travel by day or night. And the LORD did not remove the pillar of cloud or pillar of fire from its place in front of the people." People knew when to stay put and when to get up and depart as they journeyed to the land God would give them.

You can see His protection of those who chose to be obedient to His ways. You can learn about Daniel in Daniel 6. He did not change course in how he lived life with God. His career was put in jeopardy, and he was given a death sentence for not following the orders of the king. He was thrown in with the lions, and the next morning he walked out of the den unharmed. This shocked everybody because his life was spared by lions. I don't know about you, but I am in awe over the faith that people like Daniel had in the Bible.

The book of Jonah tells how he survived being in the belly of a whale for three days, all because he saw how foolish he had been for not listening to God and trying to hide from Him. God heard his confession deep in the bowels of the whale and rescued him so that he could start anew. This shows that God is forgiving and forever loving. I hope you are catching a glimpse of how God is committed to us.

Think about why God placed Jonah inside a whale. Jonah chose to not listen to what God was telling him to do, so he ran and hid. I don't know about you, but I am guilty of this. Despite our hiding, when we choose to turn and lend our ear to God, He removes us from our hiding places, wipes us off, and says, "Let's try this again."

God is the God of second chances.

In Daniel 3, three brothers were impervious to the heat of the flames because God was with them when they refused to worship the king. Go ahead and read this chapter, which is very intense. The king was very full of himself and wanted everyone to worship him. He believed he had great power such that he could control everyone and everything. Anyone who chose to disobey by not bowing to the king's gold statue was to be burned in a fiery furnace.

You can learn from these three brothers, Shadrach, Meshack, and Abednego. They were respected men who Nebuchadnezzar had put in charge of one of his provinces. Check out their faith in God. They chose to not follow the king's decree to worship him. They didn't need to when they had God, the King of the universe. They didn't need anyone else. Even in the face of death by fire, they knew that God would save them. *If God didn't, that was okay too.* They knew whom they belonged to! God is calling us to this same level of trust. He wants us to believe this same way.

Read about Noah in Genesis 6-9 and think about why God had to do what He did. Many of you are familiar with the story of Noah's Ark. The whole world went so far off the deep end that in Genesis 6:6 we read that God was sorry for making man. As I sit and work on this book during the COVID-19 pandemic, I wonder; is God sorry for how we are today? Is He needing to stop us in our tracks and quarantine us? Lord, may we hear what You want us to know.

We know He won't flood the earth again. He promised that to us in Genesis 9:12-17. And we know God keeps His promises. But will we learn and make the necessary changes so that God can heal His land as we live more simply for a short time? I think we have forgotten who owns this land. We treat it like it is ours, and we think we have the right to live how we want to. We all need a shift in our thinking and, dare I say, a kick in the pants so that we can start living in accordance with the truth that the earth belongs to God.

Despite the waywardness of man, God remains faithful and loving, for He is committed to us. He offers us a way to be reconciled with Him, though the price was steep. Neither man's wisdom, strength, nor his money can alleviate the debt that has accrued. Man is helpless to save himself. Our loving God made the ultimate sacrifice by allowing His Son, who is God Himself, to become a human being. God loves His people to the point of risking Himself.

Remember free will? God allows man to choose for himself, which meant that sending His Son to earth was risky. People might not have liked him. People might have rejected Him. People did reject Him. Acts 17:27-28a says, "His purpose was for the nations to seek after God and perhaps feel their way toward Him and find Him, though He is not far from any one of us. For in Him we live and move and exist." You are to search for God. You are made to follow after Him. Once you do, you find peace and purpose and love is restored, not perfectly, but God's presence changes you, just like it did for Daniel, Noah, and so many others.

Jesus Came in Love

In His love, Jesus came to earth as a tiny infant. His birth was unique. Mary, Jesus's mother, conceived Him when the Holy Spirit came upon her. Mary became pregnant during her engagement to Joseph. Despite what it would look like, Joseph still married her. This was abhorrent in their day, to be pregnant before the wedding. Who in his right mind would believe that they had never come together before their nuptials and that the father of the baby was God? You could say that God's love *is a crazy kind of love.*

Joseph needed some encouragement and proof that his fiancé hadn't cheated on him. So, God sent him a heavenly messenger to confirm Eve's story. God wanted to make sure that Joseph could believe what was about to happen, so He gave Joseph a very clear sign. Mary and Joseph both believed and trusted God, even if their circumstances screamed "impossible." *Do you find that kind of faith to be inspiring?* I do. Joseph obeyed and married Mary despite what others thought. They lived by God's voice instead of by their own reasoning and wants.

You could gloss over this and then move on, but you should stop for a minute and think about this scenario. Would you listen to God and move forward, like Mary and Joseph, when you knew that no one, I mean no one, would believe you? Everyone thought they had consummated their relationship before the wedding. Like I said, back in biblical times, that was considered repulsive. You would be shunned for such a thing, and everyone would look down on you from that moment on.

Through the years, Jesus became the oldest of several siblings. He learned his dad's trade as a carpenter. He stood out from everyone else because He remained sinless. Only God can say that about Himself. Can you imagine having to be Jesus's sibling? Mom and Dad would always cater to Him. No matter how hard you would try, you would mess up, but your big brother wouldn't. Yeah, that wouldn't fly with me. I know that I wouldn't be nice to him. There would be one-sided, sarcastic comments coming out of my mouth, and things would have been flung at his head.

God places you in hard situations so that you can show the world His glory.

God was ready to reveal His Son to the darkened world at the age of thirty. He began to publicly reveal who Jesus was, and He wasn't quiet and shy about it. He turned life upside down for those who loved religion. Priests and Pharisees did not like Him because He had disrupted their way of doing things. Old Testament ways were what they knew, and now the New Testament was beginning to take shape.

The Pharisees added their own ideals to Old Testament truths, and people had to follow what they said the scriptures meant. This is how religion came into being. Man added his own ideals to the scriptures. People were subject to humiliation or were simply ignored if they didn't fit into the prescribed religious persona. You can read Matthew 23 and see how Jesus criticized them. Jesus came to render the

Old Testament ways inactive as He ushered in a more personal style of walking with God.

Jesus came to teach unconditional love, grace, and mercy, which was much different from the old covenant. The priests and Pharisees had a hard time letting a new guy come in and change their ways. They couldn't see beyond what they thought they knew. Jesus claiming that He was God was simply too much for them. They wouldn't let themselves see beyond what they knew. They knew the Messiah was coming, but this guy couldn't be him.

The hardest part for these religious gurus was that Jesus was very popular. He was telling people to follow Him instead of them. The Pharisees did not like that. He healed people, calmed storms, walked on water, and loved people right where He found them. *I have Good News for you. He hasn't stopped loving people.*

God never stops loving us.

There was a woman at a well who had already had five husbands, and currently she was living with a new man. Jesus happened to need a drink of water, and He asked her for some. He offered more than a simple cup of water. He shared all that He knew of her without shaming her or degrading her. He simply told her to go and sin no more.[3] The Pharisees would have shunned her publicly, but not Jesus. He showed love.

Jesus called Zacchaeus down from a tree and ate dinner at his house. As a tax collector, Zacchaeus had stolen from many people, but Jesus saw beyond his sin. He saw a misdirected man needing new direction, not chastisement from the priests and Pharisees.[4] We are the same way. We all are misdirected in one way or another, and we need a new map to follow. Jesus came to be our map.

Did the woman at the well or the tax collector deserve such kind treatment? They hadn't done anything to warrant Jesus's love. Nope.

She was living promiscuously, and he was getting richer by cheating those around him. One would think Jesus would have kept on walking and left them to their own despair. Surely Jesus, the Son of God, could find some good people to share His love with, those who deserved it. But that is not who He is. Because of sin, none of us are good. We all have "dirty" stamped on our foreheads.

Jesus's very presence washes away the "dirty" stamp. He does this when we elect to follow Him. *It's called grace.* My son shared with me the greatest definition of grace. "At its core, grace is unfair. It is giving something to someone who is undeserving of it. Jesus dying on the cross is the most just thing God could do. But it was not fair. What is fair is for humanity to spend eternity in hell. What is unfair is for God to give us a way out."

Jesus can brag about this thing called grace because He separated Himself from all other gods that man had created through history. Jesus was not created by man. He is God. He lived out who He was in a fashion that changed lives. Those who didn't like change, like the religious leaders, worked hard at silencing Him. People who felt they were good in their own eyes wanted to get rid of Him. But when you are God, no one can silence you.

That's because Jesus did something that no one had done before. He broke the sting of death. Three days after dying a horrendous death that He did not deserve, He rose up alive! This event changed history, a.k.a. His Story. This event bridged the separation between God and man.

Remember when God was forced to usher out Adam and Eve from the Garden and man was separated from God? Now, God and man are united once again. No religion on earth can have this personal unity that is eternal. There is no other god that has conquered death!

Jesus spoke three words before He dismissed His spirit and left this earth: "It is finished."[5] These three words reveal much about who God is. Jesus's last words show His affection towards you. It is unchangeable and passionate. He is committed to His creation. *It is finished* means completion. Nothing else is needed. Through Christ, your redemption is complete. You don't not have to do anything to earn God's favor. This reveals how the Trinity is completely capable of running the universe and intimately loving the world's people. Understanding this keeps me in awe and hungry for more.

Do you wonder why God puts up with you and me? Why disobedient man is still occupying the earth more than two thousand years later? Our sinful nature will not change; however, God keeps life going. Matthew 24:14 says, "And the Good News about the Kingdom will be preached throughout the whole world, so that all nations will hear it; and then the end will come." After everyone hears about Christ, He will then return to take each of us home.

After the infraction in the Garden, Adam and Eve had to leave. They had two sons, Cain and Abel. You read in scripture how jealousy got the best of Cain and he murdered his brother. You will learn more about this in chapter 5.

You see God having had enough of man's idiocy in the story of Noah. God remained faithful and committed to *one family out of all on earth* that lived for God. He spared them with an ark that they had to build, and they were laughed at by the townspeople as they built it.

Back in Noah's time, the earth never experienced rain.[6] Then it rained and rained and rained. After the flood, God told them to go and be fruitful and multiply. It is like God was saying that He was going to give man another chance.

Looking at our track record, we don't seem to learn. History is full of wars, murders, and hypocrisy. Our home on earth will be imperfect until Jesus returns to restore what was once lost. Until that day happens, we need to live like the great men and women in the Bible. They lived with one focus; their focus was pleasing God.

This commitment that God bestows on His people by having given His Son is unimaginable. Our human mind cannot grasp or understand this level of love. If God were to ask one of us to freely give one of our own children to die for mankind, we would not step up. We love each other, but not that much. However, God does. He loves us perfectly, completely, and unconditionally.

His resurrection makes way for the Holy Spirit to live within you. He talks with you and His presence is constant. Earlier in the chapter, we read about how God led His people by a pillar of fire or a cloud. This was God's way of being with His people. He had the Israelites construct a mobile tabernacle in the middle of camp. This was the dwelling place of God. No one could simply enter in and see God for himself because a high priest was needed to make payment for sins.

In the Old Testament, people had to go through a priest to talk to God, and this was only an option at certain times of the year. These Old Testament times were arduous and the rules very tedious to follow. The book of Exodus talks about the Israelites' journey. Two million people were set free from worldly bondage. God brought them to a place where they would experience His love.

For many generations, people waited for the coming Messiah. Finally, Jesus came and broke down the arduous barriers that were so easy to trip over, becoming the unconstrained liberator and allowing man to be reconciled to God.

God has much patience with His wayward children.

Jesus will make Himself known to you when you seek Him. He never hides from a heart that desires truth. Since He created you, He knows how to talk to you so that you will understand. He will reveal Himself so that you know it is Him. Each of us has a love language that God uses to speak to us. God speaks to my husband the clearest when he is out in nature. For me, journaling scripture is my attention-getter. The most direct way God speaks to us is through the Bible.

One of the things I love about Jesus is that He is always happy to hear from me. He has taught me that I am important and that He is ready and waiting to help me. His eye is always upon me. Psalm 32:8 states, "The LORD says, 'I will guide you along the best pathway for your life. I will advise you and watch over you.'" Jesus has never left my side, ever.

The Butterfly

The death of my father was extremely hard on my mother. My father had heart issues, and at the age of seventy-four, he passed away after being ill for nine years. After his stroke at the age of sixty-five, Mom had taken care of him. Eventually, his needs became too great, and she had to make the heart-wrenching decision to put him in a nursing home. She went every day and tended to his needs.

This was a time of emotional wrestling for my mom as she came to realize that their plans for retirement were never going to happen. Retirement had been their gold at the end of their rainbow. They had wanted to travel, but my dad's health didn't warrant that. Although they were blessed with many years of marriage as well as raising eight children and experiencing grandchildren, Mom felt robbed of their golden season in life.

Jesus is our freedom fighter.

Both of my parents had worked their whole lives. Although my parents didn't attend college, my dad worked hard at managing a co-op grocery store where my mom took care of the books. She was great at math and accounting. They never experienced a windfall of any kind that would have put them on easy street, but my mom would say that they had always had enough. They managed their money well and my siblings and I never went without.

Despite her feeling of loss and loneliness over my dad, God never left my mom's side. The butterfly became a symbol of His love and His presence. In various and unusual places, she would see a butterfly and know that Dad was visiting her. I really don't know if it was my dad or God giving her comfort, but whichever it was, God showed His love to her. It is heartwarming to know that His love is so detail-orientated. It perfectly meets the needs of our hearts.

After Mom moved on from this life, I experienced seeing butterflies at various times. When I am out walking the dog, a butterfly will flutter around me, follow for a time, and then depart. It warms and comforts my heart to know that it is her or God comforting me.

Our son was a student athletic trainer for the University of Minnesota Gophers during college. He was able to get a couple tickets for each home game, and since Rob couldn't join me for the first game, my friend Renae came along. We were sitting in the corner section on the home team's side on a beautiful early-fall day when suddenly a butterfly flew around us. What was a butterfly doing inside a football stadium? It made me chuckle, and I told Renae that my mom was here to watch Alex. I texted Alex and told him that Grandma was here. The love of God is so tender and caring that He gives of Himself consistently and in such delicate ways.

God provides for our every need.

God would also reveal His presence to me in other ways. While Rob and I were adjusting to wedded bliss, we had much to learn about each other and God. I quickly discovered that God would always faithfully meet me in my struggles. I would be in my bedroom needing some alone time, and the sunlight would hit just right through the window and form a very prominent cross. This was one of the first ways that God taught me about His presence. I knew I wasn't alone and that He saw me.

Another time, my sister was visiting, and we were out walking near my neighborhood, chatting away like sisters do. As we ventured down the hill on the dirt road, we noticed two clouds coming together and forming a cross. It was plain as day. We had to stop in awe over His Glory and how He revealed His presence. It was like He was confirming what we were sharing with one another and our time together. God's intimate love is incredible and heartwarming.

God Says That I Am Breathtaking

In my early days, I struggled with who I was. I was very insecure and unsure of myself. I did not like the reflection in the mirror. There was a discrepancy between how I saw myself and how others saw me. I still struggle, unfortunately, but I know what to do when I get confused about my identity. *I talk with God, and He refocuses my eyes upon who I am in Him.* He restores me as I read and believe scripture on who He says I am.

One particular day, God refocused my image of myself. I would read from "The Daily Bread" for guidance and growth in God, and one morning, the devotional read, "A well-spoken word speaks volumes." That encouraged me, and I laid it down on my bed and went about the rest of my day tending to my children.

That afternoon, we went to Target to pick up odds and ends. While in the baby section, a middle-aged man with thinning hair and glasses came up to me and kindly said, "I am sorry to bother you, but I have got to tell you that you are breathtaking." Now, let me tell you, no one has ever come up to me to say anything like that. He left me speechless for a moment.

Needing a minute, I thought, "What planet did you just fall from?" Blushing, I managed to fumble my words together, and I think

I said thank you. "Well, uh, I'm sorry, but I am happily married," is what came stuttering out as I felt for my left hand to touch my wedding ring. Wouldn't you know it, I had left the house without any jewelry on. I smiled sheepishly. He told me to not be sorry, and he apologized for embarrassing me; then he departed. The rest of the day, I walked on cloud nine.

I was in a bit of a daze, a happy daze, as I drove home. As soon as I got home, I had to call Rob. "You will never guess what happened." I explained the story, all giddy, of course, and I loved my husband's response.

"Well, he found out what I have already known." I love that man.

I had to call a couple friends to relive that life-changing moment. I eventually went into the bedroom and noticed "The Daily Bread" laying on the bed from that morning. I picked it up and reread, "A well-spoken word speaks volumes." "Wow, Lord," I thought, "You had that man come and tell me that You think I am breathtaking." My heart was forever changed. His eye is always upon me.

I want you to know that you are breathtaking to God!

God is committed to me, and He is with you also. He continually lets me know that He sees me and He hears me. He continues to pursue my heart and woos me to fall in love with Him all the more. On that day, he was undoing the lies that I believed about myself.

Psalm 40:1-5 speaks of God loving His children in a way that causes them to fall in love with Him. "I waited patiently for the LORD to help me, and He turned to me and heard my cry. He lifted me out of the pit of despair, out of the mud and the mire. He set my feet on solid ground and steadied me as I walked along. He has given me a new song to sing, a hymn of praise to our God. Many will see what He has done and be amazed. They will put their trust in the LORD." These verses describe His committed love.

Are you struggling with your identity in Christ? Write down these verses on a notecard and place it where you can see it throughout your day, *and as you read them, believe them.*

God wants to do more for you than you can imagine. Ephesians 3:20 says, "Now all glory to God, who is able, through His mighty power at work within us, to accomplish infinitely more than we might ask or think." Reread that. God wants to do an amazing new work within you. What if? What if you handed over your doubts and fears and allowed Him to rearrange things or remove any clutter that keeps you bogged down? What if you let Him love you? What positive could come from that?

There was a woman during Jesus's lifetime who experienced His love, and it radically healed her! She had suffered physically and socially for twelve years, which made her unclean in society. No doctors could help her. In her loneliness, she heard about Jesus, and she believed He could heal her. What else did she have to lose? Nothing and no one on earth could help her.

Moving through the crowds around Him, she was able to get close enough to touch His robe. By that simple touch and having faith, power was released, and she was healed! You can read about this example of love in three different places in the Bible: Mark 5, Matthew 9, and Luke 8. Her act of faith shows that when you take a small step towards Jesus, He runs towards you, giving all of Himself. Nothing is held back. He truly loves you deeply in a way that leaves you changed from the inside out.

Chapter Four

HAVING GOOD INTENTIONS

"So, the trouble is not with the law, for it is
spiritual and good. The trouble is with me, for
I am all too human, a slave to sin."
— Romans 7:14

Wе have been learning how God is committed to His creation, and we have seen how man isn't so great at living
committed to Him. It is within us to seek and find. Jeremiah 31:33 says, "'But this is the new covenant I will make with the
people of Israel on that day,' says the Lord. 'I will put my instructions
deep within them, and I will write them on their hearts. I will be their
God and they will be my people.'" Yet, history reveals how man has
a hard time with commitment. We like to set up our own parameters

and control our surroundings. Remember in the Garden when the serpent enticed Eve to make her own decisions? She fell for it, Adam fell for it, and we fall for it. Since then, God's intended life for man has been marred, and every generation has its pitfalls because of it.

Sin is the problem that we all struggle with. Romans 7:14-20, 23-25 describes why we get entangled so easily. "The trouble is not with the law, for it is spiritual and good. The trouble is with me, for I am all too human, a slave to sin. I don't really understand myself, for I want to do what is right, but I don't do it. Instead, I do what I hate. But if I know that what I am doing is wrong, this shows that I agree that the law is good. I am not the one doing wrong; it is sin living in me that does it. And I know that nothing good lives in me, that is, my sinful nature. I want to do what is right, but I can't. I want to do what is good, but I don't. I don't want to do what is wrong, but I do it anyway. But if I do what I don't want to do, I am not really the one doing wrong; it is sin living in me that does it. But there is another power within me that is at war with my mind. This power makes me a slave to the sin that is still within me. Who will free me from this life that is dominated by sin and death? Thank God! The answer is in Jesus Christ our Lord."

We all struggle with this war within ourselves. What is hard for one person may not be an issue with another. We all vary in the things that ensnare us. And these differences cause us to compare and judge one another. We like to esteem ourselves with pride in our own strengths, while we aren't as understanding with others. Hospitality, for example, comes easily for me. While I enjoy it, another may panic at the thought of having to cook a meal and clean the house to have people over.

Fear and drudgery make their presence known while feelings of ineptitude cause us to feel less than we really are. We focus on what we lack or don't have. I wish I could sing. I wish I had skin that would tan easily. I wish for this, I wish for that. Satan dangled wishful thinking before Eve, and he dangles wishful thinking before you and me as well.

Lessons Learned in the Wilderness

We can look again in the book of Exodus and see Moses leading the Israelites from Egypt to the Promised Land. It was an eleven-day journey that took forty years. The Israelites were finally free from harsh bondage of the Egyptians, and their dreams became reality when they were set free to depart and go to the place God had promised them. They waited on God for a very long time, and He finally answered their prayers through Moses. Freedom and sweet relief from slavery were finally at their doorstep. One would think that they would be grateful for their new journey, but that is not the case. It did not take long for them to forget what God was leading them away from.

We forget, then complain, then wish to go back.

Like the Israelites, we forget too. We tire easily, then complain. We are creatures of comfort, aren't we? The unknown brings on fear, and we resist and tend to return to what is familiar—even if that means going back to captivity.

Think of a controlling habit you would like to break but can't or don't want to. You lack perseverance, and if you are like me, you don't yield to what you should do. We all battle some sort of nemesis. For me, sugar is a downfall. Self-control goes right out the window when something sweet is around. My first thought: I will begin tomorrow.

To help the Israelites understand and learn that He is God, He sent them on a roundabout way through the wilderness toward the Red Sea. Exodus 13:17 says that if the people were faced with a battle, they might have changed their minds and returned to Egypt. Whether it was an Israelite back in biblical times, or you and I today, we are shortsighted and will return to what we are so desperately trying to be free from.

Dieting is a perfect example. You tell yourself to cut back on eating junk food. Then doesn't it seem like junk food is everywhere? I can tell myself not to eat sugar. That night, Rob will come home with Girl Scout Cookies from work. Then the doorbell will ring, and I will find girls selling more cookies. I don't know about you, but I cave easily.

Despite your lack of commitment, God remains faithful to you. He knew what the Israelites needed beforehand and set their course accordingly. He wanted them to learn to depend on Him. He wants you to depend on Him for all things. Next time you find yourself in a situation that is frustrating you, let God work in you. He will bring good out of difficult situations.

God allows times of wilderness to come into your days. These are usually trying times when you may question if God really cares. They could be dark times in which you think He isn't listening. It is easy to rationalize that He hates you or that perhaps you are not worthy. But nothing could be farther from the truth.

If you are in the wilderness and feeling lost or despondent, God is near. Although you step away, God will get your attention, for His grace warrants tough love. He allows hardships so that you can learn to look up at Him and seek His help. I can promise you that there is a light at the end of the tunnel. God is helping you to remove your sins and replace them with Himself. He is helping you to become less about you and more about Him. Keep looking up, and He will lead you out. You will thank Him later when you gain clarity on a situation that is befuddling you.

God gave the book of Proverbs as an instructional guide to daily living. In Proverbs 3:5-6, King Solomon penned these words, "Trust in the LORD with all your heart; do not depend on your own understanding. Seek His will in all you do and He will show you which path to take." He wants you to let Him lead your life. You will always be in the right place at the right time when you reside on His path. Proverbs was written so that you can be encouraged daily. There are thirty-one chapters in Proverbs—one for each day of the month—in which you can see His faithfulness and provision for your every need.

The Enemy's Tactics

We now understand more clearly how society has been flawed since Adam and Eve. Every generation of people have their own issues, and one would think that by the twenty-first century, we would have it figured out. Disobedience from God has been running amok ever since, and the choices that man makes have not changed. Wealth, power, and food are three areas that man struggles with.

Why do I say this? Look at the example of Jesus. In Matthew 4, the Spirit led Jesus into the wilderness to be tempted by the devil. The devil tested him during a forty-day-and-night fasting time that would make Jesus hungry, tired, and weak. Remember, Jesus experienced life on earth in a human body. This makes him perfectly empathetic to your needs. He understands why you get cranky and tired or feel weary and exhausted.

1. Satan tested Jesus with food by asking Him to turn stones into bread. It was like he was enticing Jesus to eat Girl Scout Cookies.
2. Satan then tested Him by telling Him to jump off the highest point of the temple if He was the Son of God. Satan wanted to see His power.
3. Satan took Jesus to the peak of a very high mountain, showed Him all of his kingdoms, and asked Jesus to bow to him. Satan thought that he owned the world, and he offered to give it all to Jesus.

While God created the earth, Satan has ownership of the earth right now, and he was willing to give Jesus the wealth of the world. In his pride, Satan thinks he can outsmart God, and he thinks that he really owns what God created. It would be good for us to remember that Satan is not very smart. Because of Jesus, he is a defeated foe.

God allowed these tests to show you that Jesus is capable of handling all the issues that we toil with daily. He has the power to overcome whatever lies before you. Jesus quoted scripture to combat Satan's lies. This is how you are to combat his lies. Satan's power is broken when you speak truth, God's truth. You render him powerless, and he has to flee. This shows how vital it is to know the Bible. *You can't afford to not know it.* You can also cripple Satan when you play praise music and worship God. God gives you tools to help outsmart the enemy. In your arsenal, you have God's Word and worship music.

It is easy to tell how people are being deceived by the very same things that Satan tried to trip up Jesus with. The love of food, the chase after wealth, and the craving for importance are satiating families. They are consuming people in an unhealthy way. We have forgotten how precious and valuable life is.

Satan tried to get Jesus to take His eyes off of what is important and focus on earthly matters. He does the same with you. He does not have to work hard at getting people to focus on their own wants and needs.

For Satan, the easiest ploy is to keep people from focusing on God first. He sets half-truths in willing ears. Just believe—believe in God, believe in Jesus, believe in goodness, believe in something that you connect with—and all will be well. Everything works itself out and everyone will go to heaven. The problem with this is it is not the whole truth. It is not the gospel.

Remember how Satan experienced the harmony of the Trinity before he was kicked out of heaven? He believes Jesus. Satan and his demons tremble with fear over Christ. They understand who He is.

Read what the Bible says about Satan and his demons:

James 2:19 says, "You say you have faith, for you believe that there is one God. Good for you! Even the demons believe this, and they tremble in terror."

Mark 1:23-24 says, "Suddenly, a man in the synagogue who was possessed by an evil spirit began shouting, 'Why are you interfering with us, Jesus of Nazareth? Have you come to destroy us? I know who you are, the Holy One sent from God!'"

Mark 1:34 says, "So Jesus healed many people who were sick with various diseases, and He cast out many demons. But because the demons knew who He was, He did not allow them to speak."

Mark 3:11 says, "And whenever those possessed by evil spirits caught sight of Him, the spirits would throw them to the ground in front of Him shrieking, 'You are the Son of God!'"

Mark 5:7 says, "With a shriek, he screamed, 'Why are you interfering with me, Jesus, Son of the Most High God? In the name of God, I beg of you, don't torture me!'" Luke 8:28 speaks the same thing.

Acts 19:15 says, "But one time when they tried it, the evil spirit replied, 'I know Jesus.'"

Luke 4:41 says, "Many were possessed by demons, and the demons came out at His command shouting, 'You are the Son of God!' But because they knew He was the Messiah, He rebuked them and refused to let them speak."

Luke 10:17 says, "When the seventy-two disciples returned, they joyfully reported to Him, 'Lord, even the demons obey us when we use your name!'"

Matthew 8:16 says, "That evening many demon-possessed people were brought to Jesus. He cast out the evil spirits with a simple command, and He healed the sick."

Let me reiterate an important truth: *Satan believes Jesus*. Disobedience caused Satan to forfeit a seat in the heavenly realms. You will forfeit eternal life if you don't walk obediently. Satan knows Jesus is the Savior, but He is not Lord to him.

Satan is playing a very destructive game. Yes, you have to believe in God and in Jesus, but there is more. Jesus needs to become the Lord of your life. You need to trust God and let the Holy Spirit lead. He will help you live out scripture. The ruler of this world does not want you to discover and obey truth. If just believing is all that is needed to obtain eternal life, then the serpent would be in heaven. We know he isn't as he is not obedient to God. We won't be in heaven either if we aren't obedient. This is the greatest tragedy of man, missing eternal life.

From Birth to Blessedness

Obedience to God is man's biggest obstacle. Each of us is born as a small, helpless baby. In the womb, you are totally dependent on your mother until you are evicted to live on your own. Other than breathing, you need someone to take care of you. You learn quickly that someone has to feed, bathe, clothe, change, touch, hold, and love you, and you begin to learn that life is all about you.

From birth, our needs are met, and we are the center of attention. No wonder we balk at walking obediently with God. We are encouraged to become independent, which starts with walking and feeding ourselves. Then potty-training, school, extracurricular activities, religion, and "what do you want to be when you grow up?" As we reach each milestone, we are celebrated. It becomes engrained that *life is about me, myself,* and *I.*

God created life to begin this way, and it is the parents' job to teach right from the crib that life centers around God and Jesus. You learn, grow, develop, and respond to the world that you live in but always with an eternal perspective allowing God to lead, shape, and mold your thinking. Unfortunately, life doesn't happen quite this way. Priorities get shuffled around to where God isn't in the center. Your life become the center, and you relegate God to the backseat.

Walking with God is like riding a bike. Are you steering or is God? You must pedal and move forward, but God is leading the way. You are meant to be God-focused, not self-focused. If life is good, who needs God? If you struggle, you try to fix it with options that are around you. When you are desperate, you decide that maybe God can help you, and you finally ask Him for it.

Many of us were not taught to know Jesus from birth. Despite this, I have great news! No matter your age or your background, He wants to share life with you from this day forward. God will use your birth story, your family history, and all the good and bad in between for His Glory. No one has a perfect beginning, but His love is mighty enough to turn us into sights of beauty.

Psalm 139:17-18 says, "How precious are your thoughts about me, O God. They cannot be numbered. I can't even count them; they outnumber the grains of sand. And when I wake up, you are still with me!" Stop and think about this verse. *This verse says that God is always thinking about you.*

Let's look at Psalm 36:5-9: "Your unfailing love, O LORD, is as vast as the heavens; your faithfulness reaches beyond the clouds. Your righteousness is like the mighty mountains, your justice like the ocean depths. You care for people and animals alike, O LORD. How precious is your unfailing love, O God. All humanity finds shelter in the shadow of your wings. You feed them from the abundance of your own house, letting them drink from your river of delights. For you are the fountain of life, the light by which we see." You are so complete in Him. You can relax and fall right into His arms, knowing that He will catch you.

Jeremiah 9:23-24 says, "Don't let the wise boast in their wisdom, or the powerful boast in their power, or the rich boast in their riches. But those who wish to boast should boast in this alone: that they truly know me and understand that I am the LORD who demonstrates unfailing love and who brings justice and righteousness to the earth and that I delight in these things. I, the LORD, have spoken.'" God wants you to truly know Him.

Jesus speaks pertinent words to you in John 10:27-30. "My sheep listen to my voice; I know them, and they follow me. I give them eternal life and they will never perish. No one can snatch them away from me, for my Father has given them to me, and He is more powerful than anyone else. No one can snatch them from the Father's hand. The Father and I are one." Notice how safe you are under His care.

Living by your five senses can hinder your walk with God. You see this in Luke 17:11-19. Ten men suffered with leprosy. Because of contamination, in their day, leprosy meant loneliness and isolation. These ten men must have heard that Jesus was coming their way. As

Jesus entered their village, from a distance they cried out, "Jesus, Master, have mercy on us!" *Jesus's simple look at them warranted His love.* He told them to go and show themselves to the priests. As they left to go do what Jesus said, they were cleansed of their illness.

Now, wouldn't you think that those ten men would make a U-turn and hightail it back to Jesus to thank Him and praise Him? We sure would like to think so. We like to think, "I would go back." But would you?

Nine of those men did what most people do, found happiness in their returned health and continued on their way. I would think that they would have been thankful, but their thankfulness was misdirected. In their self-confidence, they had expected to be healed. Only one man returned to Jesus with an exuberant heart that knew where his life had come from. Only one! He praised Jesus loudly and fell at His feet, thanking Him for what He had done. Jesus asked him, "Didn't I heal ten men? Where are the other nine? Has no one returned to give glory to God except this foreigner?"

Our human behavior must sadden God. His commitment towards us is never returned in kind. For the one man who did return, his faith healed him, inside and out. For the other nine, their outsides may have been healed, but their insides were full of "self." Nine left healed but with dead hearts. The sole returning man attained mercy, grace, and love from the One who holds life in His hands, all because he chose to see beyond his five senses. His life had now been extended beyond the grave.

We should all be so thankful for God's committed love. He refers to man as sheep that need a shepherd. Sheep wander and get lost easily. They will follow one another, even to be slaughtered. We are like sheep, and we need a shepherd to guide us.

Unconditional Pursuit

"Your beauty and love chase
after me every day of my life. I'm back
home in the house of God for the rest of my life."
— *Psalm 23:6 (Message)*

With Genesis being the first book of the Bible and the intro-duction of life, one would think that sin would show up many years later and that we would read about it deeper into the Bible. Knowing what happened with Adam and Eve in the Garden, we know this isn't so. Sin disrupted God's perfect love. Shortly after leaving Eden with shame, fear, and doubt weighing on their shoulders and sin in their hearts, God blessed Adam and Eve with two sons, Cain and Abel.

Sin does not deter His love, but it will upset the way life was intended. Back in chapter 3 we mentioned how Cain became so angry at his brother that he murdered him. You can read about it in Genesis 4. Anger and feelings of unfairness caused the murder. Could these be the root causes of all the violence we see today and have seen in the past?

Farther into Genesis, we read about another set of brothers, Esau and Jacob. You can find this story in Genesis 25:27-34. These brothers were twins. Like Cain and Abel, they had two very different personalities. Esau was an outdoorsman who loved to hunt, and Jacob was a home body with a quiet temperament. On any given day, you would find Esau out in the wilderness while Jacob was home cooking. After an exhausting day in the woods, Esau came home starving, and the aroma of Jacob's stew made him even more famished.

Before moving on with the story, let's gather some information on these brothers. Esau was born first. This means that he had the birthright from his father. A birthright is a double portion of one's father's estate. Jacob would get a single portion. Receiving one's birthright back then was a big deal, but it wasn't to Esau. He was careless and hungry for worldly things.

In Hebrews 12:6, Esau is referred to as godless. In Philippians 3:19, his god was his appetite. Esau enjoyed the tangible side of life more than the spiritual side. Jacob, on the other hand, was more spiritual. He allowed his emotions to control him. You will see that he had a conniving side. Jacob saw a perfect opportunity to take matters into his own hands. Whenever anyone takes matters into their own hands, trouble usually arises.

Let's return to the story. After coming in from working, Esau barked at his brother, "I'm starved. Give me some of that red stew."

"All right," Jacob replied, "but trade me your rights as the firstborn son."

**Kingdom work will
continue until Jesus
returns to make
things right.**

"Look, I'm dying of starvation." said Esau. "What good is my birthright to me now?" Esau swore an oath and handed over his birthright to his twin brother, all for a bowl of stew.

While you may be thinking that that was dumb of Esau and selfish of Jacob, I want you to look at their behavior more closely. Both brothers were guilty of sin. One was living for himself and enjoyed what satisfied him in the moment, and the other stepped over God's boundaries and took matters into his own hands to receive the birthright. One lived ignorantly towards God's ways, and the other thought he would help God out by taking action himself instead of accepting his place in the family lineage.

We see that they are ordinary brothers going about their days. We know that they came from an important lineage. Jacob and Esau were grandsons to Abraham. Abraham was the Father of Israel, which means that God was using Abraham and his lineage to fulfill His plan to save man. It is through Jesus that God would save man, and Jesus was a descendant of Abraham, Isaac, and Jacob.

God is committed to loving man amidst sin and stupidity. Sin does not deter His love. *I love how God used imperfect humans to fulfill His plan to redeem mankind.* This is a great encouragement because He has not changed. God can use me and He can use you to fulfill His mission. Even with imperfections, *God can use us for His glory. May we never forget that.*

Esau didn't care about his spiritual heritage, and Jacob was a manipulator like his mother. Keep reading to see how Mama took care of her favorite baby boy. The behavior that we see from people in the

Bible is no different than what we see today. Aren't we guilty of behaving the same way? Don't we respond with our feelings and emotions first, which makes it easy to get careless about the spiritual side of life? We take sides, have favorites, and keep our eyes focused horizontally around us instead of vertically, where God comes first and everything else in life comes after.

The twins' father was nearing the end of his life and wanted to bless Esau with his birthright. The boys had never told their dad what had transpired at the dinner table. Mom and her younger son cooked up a plan to convince Isaac that Jacob was Esau so Isaac would bind the covenant with Jacob. See, I told you that Mom got involved. After it was too late, Esau realized what was at stake, and he became very angry with his brother for deceiving him and their dad.

Again, Mom came to the rescue for her favorite son and had him flee to safety. You can read the entirety of this story in Genesis 27. You may have thought that you are the only one who comes from a dysfunctional family. Nope. We all have issues, shortcomings, and sins that need to be brought into the light of Christ where *His love will embrace and change us without condemnation.*[1]

So, what can you learn from this? When you focus your appetite on the things in this world, you lose sight of who you are in God. Your senses get dulled to what is important. In Christ, you inherit the Kingdom of God. You have a birthright. You are a firstborn child in God's eyes, but you can easily be duped by the enemy or forget who you are. It may be time to look at yourself in the mirror again and ask God to give you a pep talk.

Not long after sin invaded the world, anger, unfair treatment, jealousy, manipulation, deceit, favoritism, and overstepping spiritual boundaries appeared. However, amidst the troubles that we stir up for ourselves, God remains who He is and continually seeks to show us the right path to take.

**God pursues you despite
what you have done.**

Let's go back and learn more about Cain and Abel. God tried to reason with Cain before the first murder occurred and asked him why he was so angry. "Why do you look so dejected? You will be accepted if you do what is right. But if you refuse to do what is right, then watch out. Sin is crouching at the door, eager to control you. But you must subdue it and be its master."[2] You see God reaching out before trouble brews. He is always watching over His creation and directing you to do the right thing. Cain, unfortunately, didn't heed divine direction.

Empty Chaos

When our lives follow what the world dictates, we won't heed either. Our schedules are packed full of mindless shopping, fitness training, kids' sports and activities, and so many other blurry diversions that keep our eyes dim and our ears closed to the reality around us. As long as we don't stop and think about what we are doing, the illusion of happiness remains intact. Some even add church to the

empty chaos. We go about our days as we see fit, keeping God at a distance. We shout out a quick prayer when we need Him for something. Remember the nine men healed from leprosy? And do I dare say that the pandemic of 2020 could be a wake-up call from God? It's time for us to slow down and reflect.

**God is not a genie. He is
not here to please you.**

Could it be that God is allowing so much turmoil like cancer, devastating storms, the foolishness of governments, and violence escalating to such lawlessness all because He needs to take drastic measures to get people to redirect their sight upward? It is so easy, especially in the United States, *to live like we are guaranteed a tomorrow*. Our immediate needs are met when our accounts have money in it, we freely use a credit card or two, homes are comfortable, stores are stocked with a variety of food, apparel, and anything we want, and there's the convenience of gas on every corner and a car to take us anywhere. When disruptions occur, we cry out, "Woe is me."

We have sense enough to know that some habits are not good for us, but we don't want to stop and change. We know what smoking does to our lungs, but we continue to light up. We know alcohol impairs judgment, but we still get behind the wheel. Our consciences exude an uncomfortable feeling when we look at something that is not appropriate, but we look anyway. Ease and comfort steal much from us, and a divided society is a big indicator of the sickness plaguing our land.

Cancer Is No Match for God

Most of us have felt the pain of cancer. My mom, sister-in-law, and brother died from cancer, all within nine years. It is difficult to watch someone agonize over such a vicious illness. Cancer disrupts everything. Much is taken away, and hope is challenged or lost. But with God it isn't, and I am so thankful. In May 2017, I received the call. After having a second mammogram and a biopsy, the results showed cancer.

The rug came flying out from under my feet as I heard the news. A numbness enveloped me, along with a darkness that felt terribly frightening. This is what ran through my mind, "Where can I hide? This can't be happening. Are you kidding me?" My life changed in an instant, *and I am thankful that I knew what to do and where to go.*

I knew God had me. Cancer did not surprise Him. He was already fighting the war that was raging inside me. I had come to know God personally, so I knew I could trust Him. I had faith that God was going to help me get through whatever I was going to face.

When life becomes numb, startling, and scary, it is good to know what to do. Because I learned who God is in the Bible, I went straight to Him. I dove headfirst into His Word. It is my safe place where I find unconditional love, acceptance, peace, a listening ear, and an undeniable comfort of knowing that all will be well.

Now, this doesn't mean that I wasn't anxious and fearful, because I was. I hate the unknown, and my mind went racing with all the scenarios that could happen. Thankfully, I knew what to do with my anxiety and fear. I read my Bible, I talked with God, I read some more, and I journaled what was racing through my head along with truth from His Word. And in these activities, I found peace: the peace that surpasses all understanding.

From the first time I called on God, God has made me feel welcomed. I don't know where you are at spiritually, but I can tell you with the utmost confidence that He will welcome you and that He will be thrilled that you are looking at Him, no matter how scuffed up you are. We all come to God disheveled. Nothing in your life would make him turn away. Nothing.

The very night after receiving the doctor's call, my neighbors came over to see me. They brought me a journal with my favorite verse on the cover, Isaiah 41:10. What made this special is that Mike and Cindy did not know that that was my life verse. They didn't know that I journaled. It is heartwarming to know that God cares intimately for you. He ministers perfectly, through His Spirit or through other people. He wants you to know how special and loved you are. So, when God is prompting you to serve another person, do it. You will be a blessing.

I know this for a fact. As I was growing and maturing in my faith walk while living in Oklahoma City, I would send letters to my siblings. As I wrote to Kathy, the sister closest to me in age, I realized that I would write out what it means to receive Christ and follow Him. Little did I know that she would keep my letters. Within a month after our father's passing, we chatted on the phone, and she mentioned how she was understanding spiritual things. It was like the lightbulb had clicked on. She added that she took out my letters and reread them and that *they had made sense now*. So, you see, when God prompts you to do something or say something, do it! He will use it for His glory when the timing is right.

This "bump in the road," as I called my diagnosis, came in the middle of writing this book. As I journaled in the first week or so after finding out, God did not have me focus on my cancer. He had me focus on how He was going to use me because of the cancer and gave me a song to sing—"The Lion and the Lamb," by Big Daddy Weave. I sang the chorus confidently, "Who can stop the Lord Almighty?" over and over and over and over. It's good to confirm to your soul that someone has your life under control. This is the Rock that we stand on, a foundation that is secure.

I had DCIS breast cancer that was caught early at stage 0. I am thankful for doctors and mammograms. Here is what I know, ladies: get your mammograms every year. Any men reading this, get the women in your family to go and get it done. I was faithful with mine, but my latest one revealed calcification spots that turned out to be cancerous.

Since it was caught early, I chose to have a lumpectomy, which meant having radiation too. After surgery, I received the results showing that I hadn't gotten clear margins. I found this to be difficult. The cancer was still there. Rob and I were angry and depressed as we processed the next steps. I remember that weekend being rainy, which was quite fitting for how we were feeling.

God meets you smack dab in the middle of your crisis.

Doctors will say to do what is best for you, physically and mentally. Do you want to know how hard that is? How was I supposed to know what was best? There is a mental anguish that goes along with making tough decisions, so I went to my safe place, right into His lap, with His Word in my arms. He literally kept my mindset sane and joy in my heart. God's love is a hard one to describe. It is a crazy love that defies circumstances.

Here is how God spoke to my soul as I processed my next steps. He spoke to me from Psalm 116:1-9: "I love the Lord because He hears my voice and my prayer for mercy. Because He bends down to listen, I will pray as long as I have breath!" God spoke to me, "Carol, this cancer diagnosis—I am having you face your fear . . . of doctors, sicknesses, the unknown, death perhaps . . ." I kept reading. "Death wrapped its ropes around me; the terrors of the grave overtook me; I saw only trouble and sorrow. Then I called on the name of the Lord: 'Please, Lord, save me!' How kind the Lord is! How good He is! So merciful this God of ours! The Lord protects those of childlike faith; I was facing death, and He saved me. Let my soul be at rest again, for the Lord has been good to me. He has saved me from death, my eyes from tears, my feet from stumbling, and so I walk in the Lord's presence as I live here on earth!"

God met me right in the middle of His truths so that I could trust and know that He was carrying me. He is this way every single perfect time. He never ceases to amaze me. God wants to be your constant in life. Let Him delight you in ways that will satisfy your soul. And when troubles arise, you will know where to go and who to look to.

Remember, God is committed. Even in the darkest corners of this world, He is there. Even in the midst of bad choices and wrong thinking, He is there. He has never left His children, ever. Psalm 139:7-11 says, "I can never escape from your Spirit. I can never get away from your presence. If I go up to heaven, you are there; if I go down to the grave, you are there. If I ride the wings of the morning, if I dwell by the farthest oceans, even there your hand will guide me, and your strength will support me. I could ask the darkness to hide me and the light around me to become night."

Hard Times in Life Are No Match for God

Hopefully you are grasping the truth that God is not the problem when life goes awry. We are the ones who leave, doubt, and go our own way in making choices, yet we find His love remains. Remember how God told Adam and Eve the rules of living in the Garden? Everything was permissible except for the one tree. And we know what they did. We are no different, are we? We are like little children who are told to not touch something. What do we do? We touch, over and over and over again.

We are the ones who need daily wake-up calls to start each day, one from the alarm clock and one from the Holy Spirit. One is needed to physically get these aging bodies up and moving, and the other one to get our mindset geared with God so we can meet the needs of His day. Our tendency is to be physically prepared and to let our mindset just follow along however it feels. We go about our days so routinely that we don't stop and think how every good thing is from God.[3] *If we would stop and really think about that, we would see more of Him in our midst and hear more from Him.*

Illnesses uproot man's routine. Fires uproot man's possessions. Civil unrest uproots man's security. Earthquakes and tornadoes uproot man's safety. The lack of morals uproots man's trust. What causes your foundation to crumble and crack?

Jesus says in Matthew 7:26-27, "But anyone who hears my teaching and doesn't obey it is foolish, like a person who builds a house on sand. When the rains and floods come and the winds beat against that house, it will collapse with a mighty crash." I would think everyone can say that life is hard and unpredictable—a sudden job loss or a health diagnosis or a car accident or your basement flooding. How do you handle the ups and downs of life?

While I pondered my next steps after my surgeries, others around me were pondering their lives too. A man was living day-to-day, waiting to get his call for new lungs. Parents were agonizing over finding their one-year-old daughter head down in a bucket of water; after several weeks in the hospital, she left this earth. Parents to a newly adopted boy weren't having the joyous family time they dreamed of; this mama ended up in the hospital with a severe infection one week after bringing her newborn son home—her healing was drawn out into months. A friend was having uncontrolled seizures. These are issues that cause many to question: *where is God?*

It seems like this world is always shaking things up and giving us new norms. Losing a part of my body was going to be a part of my new norm. As I journaled and prayed and processed this, I realized that God is my norm. He is my constant. Thank you, Lord, in you I have security, hope, and purpose; and I am anchored in Your love.

I have to say that life is tranquil when God becomes your norm. I was able to make hard decisions with peace and clarity. Another lumpectomy really wasn't an option. So, I chose reconstruction. If I had a bi-lateral mastectomy, then I removed the chance of breast cancer returning, and since it was caught early, I *wouldn't need* radiation or chemo. That was music to my ears. So, I had the double mastectomy with reconstruction. It really wasn't that bad. It helped greatly to have a strong support system and a high pain tolerance. I give all praise and glory to God as I adjusted to a new me.

Faithful Provision

Our world offers a plethora of options when it comes to where to seek advice, and many of them are helpful, in the moment. Assistance is all around you. But God does not want to be on your list of options, He wants to be your first option. He knows you better than you know yourself. After you seek His ways and advice, He may very well lead you to an earthly option like a doctor or a friend to talk to. *The key is that He is leading you.*

We have a difficult time keeping this priority straight. We tend to love people or things more than God. This is when we get ourselves into trouble. 1 John 2:15-17 speaks so clearly of this, "Do not love this world nor the things it offers you, for when you love the world, you do not have the love of the Father in you. For the world offers only a craving for physical pleasure, a craving for everything we see and pride in our achievements and possessions. These are not from the Father but are from this world. And this world is fading away, along with everything that people crave. But anyone who does what pleases God will live forever."

God did not simply create you to leave you to your own resources. He always provides provision. We like to reduce His provisions and call them coincidences or luck. But coincidences and luck are random, and God is not random. He is purposeful with everything He does. Though you may lose your focus, He never loses His. He is El Roi, the God of Seeing. "Nothing in all creation is hidden from God. Everything is naked and exposed before His eyes and He is the one to whom we are accountable."[4]

God is unconditionally pursuing you. Before the serpent tricked Adam and Eve, life was without any flaws. After disobedience, Adam and Eve and their lineage—that's you—were separated from God for eternity because of sin. Romans 6:23 says, "For the wages of sin is death but the free gift of God is eternal life through Christ Jesus our Lord." God being separated from His people grieved Him but because He is love, He remained committed and designed a heart-wrenching way to redeem man back to Himself. He is on an unconditional pursuit of His children.

Man's Last Worst Day

"For God says, 'At just the right
time, I heard you. On the day of salvation, I helped you.'
Indeed, the 'right time' is now. Today is the day of salvation."
— 2 Corinthians 6:2

God has a plan. It is one of redemption. In the Garden, Adam and Eve's needs were met and they were surrounded by harmony, love, and understanding. Nothing weighed them down. However, from their day of disobedience when Adam and Eve departed God's Garden, they went out into the wilderness of the world wearing weighted backpacks.

They found out that life would be different. Backpacks of regret, shame, and remorse—along with guilt—were strapped to their backs, and they were ushered out into the cold, dark world. Man was on his own for the first time ever. I wonder what they thought and felt? Was it fear, loneliness, desperation—maybe confusion? They must have questioned, "How could God do this to us?" And over a two-thousand-year span, every man has struggled with these same feelings, thoughts, and questions. Satan could not be more pleased.

In my journey, I have learned that Satan's only goal *is my destruction*. Satan loathes me. All he cares about is making sure that I am not glorifying God. This is his goal for you. As long as I am not living life in a manner in which God is receiving the glory, then Satan is victorious. He gloats and grins as he throws more busyness my way and keeps me occupied to the point of exhaustion. I succumb to entertaining negative thoughts.

My relationships suffer terribly when I am unbalanced. I shut down and spew out whatever is on my mind, especially when I am tired. I get bent out of shape at little nuisances, and this leads to frustrations, short fuses, and arguments. Fights are waged and relationships suffer, and Satan seethes with satisfaction at the chaos created.

God's Amazing Son

Despite the repercussions from their disobedience, God had a plan. This plan of God's is one of peace and restoration. The one and only antidote was to offer Himself. He was willing to become like us so that He could provide a way to return to what He originally designed. The offering of Himself is the greatest sacrifice of love and commitment, and it was shown by sending His sinless and pure Son to this earth. We cannot boast of such love. We are born from imperfect people where sin gets passed down.

Jesus's birth was nothing extraordinary. Joseph and Mary had traveled to Bethlehem to register for the census that everyone had to take part in. The town was bustling. When Mary went into labor, they could not find a place to settle in except for a cave with animals. The third person of the Trinity was born where it was stinky and dirty. Joseph, Mary, and Jesus were alone with animals and dung. Nothing extravagant for God's Son. Mary delivered Jesus, born among busyness. No one noticed except a few magi and shepherds. There will be a day when Jesus will return. Will you know when it takes place? Will God find you waiting with your lamp lit? Read Luke 12:35-40 to learn what it means to have your lamp burning.

Jesus grew up and learned his father's carpentry trade. At the age of thirty, He began public ministry. He started to reveal who He was to people. People were living by the ways of the Old Testament. Jesus was now exercising His authority as the new way to walk with God. For the next three years, He revealed why God had sent Him.

Many came to believe Him, while others just couldn't wrap their minds around a simple man proclaiming to be God's Son. They had their own ideas of what God's Son should look like, so they missed out. They might have expected to see regal pomp and circumstance. I would have expected God to come down in reigning glory with gala flair like a performance at the Super Bowl, but He came with mud on His brow instead, as He was born where animals stayed.

During His three years of ministry, many got tired of hearing, "Come follow me." Despite what they saw and heard, they didn't want to. I understand this. When I don't want to do something, I dig my heels in and fight. Stubbornness causes me to miss out. I miss out because I'm fearful of change. It is easier to live in familiarity where I feel safe.

It is easier to resist, walk away, or get rid of the problem. Man opted for the third choice. Kill Jesus. Let's get rid of Him so we can go back to normal, they thought. They found that silence was golden for three days after His death. He was gone. No more Jesus. The crucifixion on Friday meant that the weekend was quiet. Finally, that nemesis was out, but *God had a plan.*

No one was prepared for what happened next. A woman close to Jesus arrived at the supposedly locked and guarded tomb on Sunday morning. In amazement, she found it open and unguarded with Jesus's body gone. Most thought His body was stolen, but to the few who believed and followed, the words of Jesus now made sense. They knew.

God Is Alive

He is alive! God defeated His nemesis. Jesus broke the bondage of death that plagues man. Redemption and restoration are now available to all people. In the following days, He revealed Himself, and He made Himself known to over five hundred people. It was time for believers to spread

The Word of God becomes clear when we walk with Christ.

His Name throughout the world, which believers have been doing ever since.

I mentioned in a previous chapter how Jesus's resurrection renders the Old Testament inactive. God ushered in a relationship-style love that is unconditional and personal. Religion's rules had been the way, up to this point, and people had had to follow the priests and religious leaders. They had needed to trust that those leaders knew what they were talking about. But now, the resurrection cancelled the need to follow the Pharisees and priests. You can commune with God yourself.

Every person now has access to God Himself. Grace and mercy are the reasons for God loving us this way. Romans 5:8 says, "But God showed His great love for us by sending Christ to die for us while were still sinners." His love freely redeems you. You are now made whole and clean with access into His presence.

When you believe, trust, and follow Jesus, today will be your last worst day on earth in respect to your soul. You become part of a family with the richest inheritance. You receive what Adam and Eve had in the Garden. Colossians 1:12-14 says, "He has enabled you to share in the inheritance that belongs to His people, who live in the light. For He has rescued us from the kingdom of darkness and transferred us into the Kingdom of His Dear Son who purchased our freedom and forgave our sins."

This was a death blow to Satan. He knows his reign on earth has an end. His demise will take place when Jesus returns, but until then, he puffs and struts around deceiving people to ignore who Christ is. He is full of hot air. His power is defeated, but he is not going down alone. Like I mentioned before, he is fully invested in our destruction. Just like he did with Eve, he lies to deceive and cause doubt so that reality is distorted.

In the United States, Satan doesn't have to try hard to deceive people. Life is comfortable—too comfortable. A poor person here is richer than in many parts of the world. Comfort brings on laziness. Comfort subdues a grateful heart. Comfort grows our appetite for more. We become entitled. When life throws unexpected curve balls, we kick and scream and blame God, asking why. This is unfair. We shouldn't have to experience this. Like Eve, we bite the apple. I have bitten it quite a few times. At first it is sweet, but the aftertaste turns bitter. I have never found it to be worth it.

Our sin can never turn God away.

We are sinful, and we are easily lured away. God's love is beyond sin. It is unconditional. Our sin can never turn His love away. When we choose to believe Jesus and follow His ways, our lives become strong, like a foundation for a building. As in Matthew 7:24-25: "Anyone who listens to my teaching and follows it is wise, like a person who builds a house on solid rock. Though the rain comes in torrents and the floodwaters rise and the winds beat against that house, it won't collapse because it is built on bedrock." Jesus is the foundation that we need to be standing upon.

Bedrock is a synonym for God Himself. The Bible refers to God as the Rock fifty-nine times. In 2 Samuel 22:2-3, David sings about God rescuing him from his enemies, "The LORD is my Rock, my fortress, and my Savior; my God is my Rock in whom I find protection. He is my shield, the power that saves me and my place of safety. He is my refuge, my Savior, the one who saves me from violence." We all need saving, and God gives us what we need for that to happen.

Without Christ, you are just existing. Eventually life ends and so will you. Jesus turns that around and gives your life eternal purpose from this day forward. The moment you say yes to Jesus Christ and follow Him, you become partakers of all that is God's.

You Have a Story to Tell

Did you know that God wants to begin a good work in you? You possess a worthiness that will make this world better. When God is within you, you have a calling that will bring glory to God as others see His light within you. Philippians 1:6 says, "And I am certain that God, who began the good work within you, will continue His work until it is finally finished on the day when Christ Jesus returns." God is so committed to you that even when you are the farthest from Him, He stands next to you. God loves you, and He wants to have a relationship with you.

You have a story to tell that the world is waiting to hear. You do not have to be famous or wealthy to have a story. You don't have to have this big transformational, saved-from-the-grip-of-death kind of story to be used by God. You may be a go-getter, adventurous, laid-back, or a simple person. Whatever

You have a message that the world needs to hear.

your style, God wants to use you to better this world.

I don't have an epic, death-defying story to amuse you with. I have a less-than-grandiose story, but God tells me that I matter and that the things I go through and learn from are going to help others. He has led me to serve and help my spouse to be his best. He led me to serve and teach my children and to be involved, for instance, by helping at their schools. He has led me to help women discover God's love through Bible study and to mentor moms of young ones through the Mothers of Preschoolers organization, known as MOPS.

I am a quiet, reserved, kind-hearted, and creative gal. I like simple things, and I am young at heart. I laugh at dumb things, and my son tells me that I have the humor of a ten-year-old boy. Put on a show like *The Muppets* and you will find me laughing hysterically. You should have seen me at Disney World watching the Muppets show. I laughed so hard that I was crying.

On the outside, I might appear like I have it all together, but inside it's a different story. I am temperamental. Psychologists may call them mood swings, but I liken my mindset to a battle zone. Depending on the situation, I may handle it positively or allow myself to be anxious and become negative. I have never tried drugs nor smoked, and I have never been drunk. Quite frankly, I don't like the taste of alcohol, so I don't drink very much. If I do, it is something very sweet.

My shyness in school may have been my lifesaver protecting me from trying dumb things in my early years. While you may be thinking "Goody Two-shoes," that's not it. I was simply too shy, and staying home was my safe place. I have always disliked my shyness, and I view it as a curse. Unfortunately, it has kept me from experiencing life. Thankfully, God has taught me to try new things. My latest adventure was ziplining through the mountains in Vancouver, British Columbia. Like I mentioned before, my favorite place has always been the amusement park. I love roller coasters because I get off the ride all pumped, knowing that I can conquer anything. As if you can't tell, I like to be thrilled over things.

I get mad, so much so that my dad's nickname for me was Pepper. Anger erupts within me, even over little things. I'm not proud to say that I have lied, and I would rather be in vacation mode than work mode. Who wouldn't? More times than not, my feelings dominate my actions. I've had to ask for forgiveness from my husband and children, and I comfort myself with food.

Now you may be thinking, "Carol, you sure are hard on yourself." No, I am not. God has led me to see who I am in my flesh, and the beautiful nature of God is that He didn't leave me there to wallow. He picked me up and helped me to see my need for a savior. He helped me to see that I am a sinner, and from there, Jesus won me over with His love.

His Love Is A Process

My last worst day was when I was thirteen-years-old. My brother shared with me the knowledge of the love of God and how Jesus had died for my sins. I remember saying yes to Jesus, and now, looking back forty-one years later, He had quite a plan for me that is still unfolding. Writing this book is my latest adventure of obedience. Yes, obedience to God

Jesus will win you over with His love.

is an adventure. Aren't we pessimistic in our human nature to think otherwise? Isn't it like Satan to downplay what God tells us so that we look elsewhere?

Think about how easy it was for Satan to downplay God's words to Eve. He used enticement to lure her away. He lures us into having fun-filled days of worldly activities. While many are good, they aren't essential when we are God's children. He distracted Eve with flattery. He flatters us with lies—anything to get our focus off of what God has said. He lies by causing downward spirals to happen within our minds so we either think too highly of ourselves or think we are not worthy. Satan's goal is to keep us unbalanced.

Yes, in my younger years, I was extremely shy. I am not exaggerating when I say that pretty much everything scared me. I don't know why. I had parents who raised me well. I was cared for and loved. I am a rule follower and a homebody who didn't cause trouble. I love routine. It is what keeps me grounded. Some thrive on the unknown and love when things change often. Not me. So, when my brother shared Jesus with me, I said yes, but I didn't fully understand the implication of what it really meant.

Through my middle and high school years, God was working in my heart. Despite not knowing the Bible very well, my heart was very aware of right and wrong. I grew up in the Lutheran faith, attended church, and went to Sunday School. I was confirmed when I was fifteen. This was a big deal as a Lutheran. I was becoming an "adult" in church. I could teach and tithe now. While understanding the outward ways of being Lutheran, my heart wasn't grounded in God's Word.

I have always loved art. There is a picture of me writing on the wall with crayons when I was two. I began drawing at a young age. I could sit for hours and create things. Along with art, I loved fashion, so I attended a college in Minneapolis for fashion design my freshman year. I was excited to combine fashion and art in a career. I lived with my brother and his family while attending school. This was the same brother who led me to Christ. I found moving to Minneapolis both exciting and scary since I came from living in a small town in Upper Michigan.

Living in the Twin Cities was the start of my learning about a relationship with Jesus. God built up my confidence as I learned the metro's bus system, started college, and made new friends. It was time to spread my wings. He planted His seeds deep within me, and those seeds were going to take root later on.

While I came from parents who believed in God and attended church, church was only a part of our life on Sundays. My brother

Dave and his wife Linda lived out God daily. Church was a person named Jesus Christ. I learned that church was inside a person rather than in a building or a denomination. The church is made up of His children who have come to believe and follow His Son. For ten months, I watched how a family lives out God's Word—not perfectly, but with love for God and grace for one another.

I graduated from fashion school with a new direction: graphic design. Being a college student short of money, I found I could move back home and attend Northern Michigan University where they had a good program that was affordable. I was reluctant, to say the least, because I loved Minneapolis. I didn't want to go back to living with Mom and Dad, but you do what you have to do, and God was working behind the scenes.

So, home is where I went. I had grown spiritually, and I did not want to lose that nor my independence. I had learned what having a relationship with God looked like. As I have matured in my walk, I have found that going back to old ways isn't a good thing when it comes to walking with God. He wants you moving forward towards maturity in Him. Believers need encouragement from fellow sojourners to stay the course. However, for me, returning home meant that I would lose that fellowship.

Remember from chapter 4 that man does not naturally follow God? My heart desired God and His Word, but I did not know what to do with it, so I drifted away from truth. The sad part is that I didn't realize how easy it was to drift away. It is so easy to go back to old ways and familiarity.

Remember the Israelites out in the wilderness heading to the Promised Land? They wanted to go back to Egypt numerous times. The unfamiliar road ahead always seems daunting. It is easier to go back or remain stagnant where you are rather than moving forward. This is why, in the Bible, Paul likens our walks with God as a race like a marathon. We keep running towards the prize, which is Jesus Himself.

My sophomore year of college was a new adventure at a new college with a new direction. While exciting and scary at the same time, I was lonely. I didn't have close friends. I was living back at home, and I yearned to have a boyfriend. I had never dated through high school. In my mind, I had believed that high school was for dating, going to homecoming dances, and prom. Since no boy had asked me to any dances or on a date, I had felt left out. I had felt ugly and unworthy.

A girl dreams of her Prince Charming coming to rescue her. I was looking for mine—or anybody that would fill an empty void in my heart. I had taken a bite of Eve's apple. I believed that to feel complete and loved, you needed a boy by your side. I cried and prayed for a boyfriend. Satan was duping me with a false identity. I was looking at my own self and trying to figure out what I needed.

On the second day of classes, I met my sister and a bunch of people from my hometown for lunch. Kathy introduced me to everyone, but one particular person stood out. His name is Robert John German. Let me tell you, he had nice hair, a shy smile, and wore a blue sweater that made his hazel eyes stand out. He smiled at me, and I smiled back.

Chapter Seven

BECOMING MORE
LIKE JESUS

*"This means that anyone who belongs to
Christ has become a new person. The old life
is gone; a new life has begun."*
— *2 Corinthians 5:17*

Rob and I met at college in 1985. As we sat in the Wildcat Den, we discovered that we liked Minneapolis, family was important, and graduating college was a priority. Rob was going to be an engineer. I had brothers who were engineers, and they had stable careers, so I knew this was a good thing.

We would walk to the library to study. Rob would tell me about deer and bear hunting, along with fishing stories. I wondered why he told me these stories, then I realized that he must like me. When I would study, he would close the book on me to get my attention. We would hang together outside between classes, and he would throw pebbles at me, and eventually he would ask me, "So, do you want to take me out sometime?"

I would reply, "Oh, maybe." I would never give him a straight answer.

Now, remember, I had received Christ only a few short years before, so I was a young believer. I had just returned from living with my brother, where I witnessed Jesus being lived out in real time. I had grown so much that first year of college, and now I was back home, resenting it, and trying to move forward in a new direction for a career. I hadn't learned how to live out Jesus's words, "Come and follow Me." You will see that was about to change. God was going to teach me.

Rob was not a believer when we met. For me, that wasn't on the top of my priority list. I was thrilled and elated that a boy finally liked me. College and a boyfriend were my priorities at age nineteen. I had found a career that I loved to pursue, and I had met Rob.

Where was God? On the back burner. I kept Him in my life, I just didn't need him to lead. At this time in my life, Jesus was my Savior but not my Lord. Life was good in my eyes. And when life is good, who needs God to lead? I am so thankful that God didn't walk away when I pursued my own agenda. God is not only faithful, He's committed too. God takes our choices, whether good or bad, and redeems them to bring Him glory.

God has never left my side, even when my stubborn mindset has led the way. If God can soften my stubbornness, He can soften you. Seriously, I mean that. God is always ready to step in, lovingly take your hand into His, and move you forward. Even severe shyness didn't deter God from showing me who I am when I walk with His Son.

While dating, Rob did attend church with me, but I wasn't about to wait until he became a believer in Christ. I wanted to get married. 2 Corinthians 6:14 says, "Don't team up with those who are unbelievers. How can righteousness be a partner with wickedness? How can light live with darkness?" I knew about this truth, but when your desires take precedence over obedience to God, you trust your own thinking. I remember telling God, "If you don't want me to marry Rob, then stop the wedding." I continued planning the wedding. I know, that wasn't the smartest way to think, but my desires and wants dictated my life at that time. *When you live by your own desires, you don't think clearly.* It is easy to take a bite of the apple that the enemy has dangled in front of you.

Your desires give way to choices, and your choices reveal what is truly in your heart. I had a void in my heart that brought out my clouded thinking. It was loneliness, something that I battle daily. As a small child, I had an imaginary friend to keep me company. As I grew, I would have expectations that my friends invite me to things. When I didn't receive an invite or I was forgotten, it devastated me. As an adult, it still stings. I do not want to be forgotten or alone; no one does.

Loneliness is crippling. It is a part of the separation anxiety you feel because of sin. You are made to be in the presence of God, and you know that God gives you Himself through His Son's sacrifice. When the Holy Spirit enters into your believing heart, you are never alone anymore. The issue that you run into is that you still live in a scuffed-up body that wants to run free. This creates a battle, of sorts. You want to live in the presence of God while still desiring to do your own thing.

Remember Isaac's sons Esau and Jacob from chapter 5? When your eyes are on yourself, you do dumb things. I let my stubborn, selfish wants dictate my actions. How easy it is when you do not take God's Word seriously to convince yourself that things are right even when they are not. Satan will use everything in his arsenal to keep you distracted and self-driven so you don't take the time to study the Bible.

God Is Amidst Life's Trials

After dating for over four years and graduating college, Rob and I married. We arrived in Puerto Vallarta, Mexico, for our honeymoon only to learn that Rob's employer had closed its doors. Picture this, we were in a foreign place, newly married, and we became jobless. I was waiting until after our wedding to find a job. Amidst our first big trial as husband and wife, God made His presence known, "Carol, don't worry, I have you." This was another one of my early lessons on learning to recognize His voice. While I held onto those words, Rob was a bit more shaken and unsure.

I am so grateful for the Holy Spirit keeping me calm and peaceful. He taught me Romans 5:3-4: "Carol, rejoice when we run into problems and trials, for we know that they help us develop endurance. Endurance develops strength of character, and character strengthens our confident hope of salvation. This hope will not lead to

God hears all of your prayers.

disappointment. For we know how dearly God loves us because He has given us the Holy Spirit to fill our hearts with His love." He has been faithful with His love towards me ever since. He is keenly aware of my situations. Whatever you are facing, God knows how to help you.

Within a few weeks, Rob and his brother got job offers with the same company. The office was located in Oklahoma City, so we took the job transfer from St. Paul and headed south. God was moving me, along with a new husband, to a place that I had never been to. He was putting me in a foreign land to teach me about Him. Have you ever been in a place that is foreign and unfamiliar? While scary, it can be the best thing to happen to you. It was for me.

Little did I realize that moving to Oklahoma City would be the start of my faith walk, where I learned how to have a relationship with

Jesus Christ. The seeds planted at my brother's house while I was in college were going to take root, grow, and flourish. I was going to learn about trust and to develop a believer's heart. Jesus was going to become my Lord.

Marrying Rob meant we were on a journey together. God led me into the unknown called Oklahoma. Abraham understood this kind of move. He followed when God spoke. Hebrews 11:8-9 speaks of who Abraham is. "It was by faith that Abraham obeyed when God called him to leave home and go to another land that God would give him as his inheritance. He went without knowing where he was going. And even when he reached the land God promised him, he lived there by faith for he was like a foreigner living in tents." I did the same but not in tents. Our first home was a one-bedroom apartment. My inheritance was a relationship with Jesus Christ, and, may I add, it has become invaluable and priceless.

The first several months was a settling-in time. Rob was adjusting to a new job, I was job hunting, and my brother-in-law was living with us for five weeks in a one-bedroom apartment. Jerry was house hunting to bring his family down from Minnesota. Meanwhile, attending church on Sunday was put on the back burner as we spent the summer adjusting to our new normal. Eventually Rob and I began attending a Lutheran church after I shared that "life isn't right when you don't go to church."

As Rob was getting acclimated to his job, I found my first job out of college at a food wholesaler's company several months after moving. God was leading in ways that I would soon discover. One discovery was my co-worker who became my dear friend.

We All Need a Timothy by Our Side
Meeting Cecilia was a confirmation that God was working in my life. She became my Timothy. This is a reference to someone coming alongside and encouraging you in your faith. Timothy was taught by

the Apostle Paul to help others in their faith journeys. We became close and began attending Bible Study Fellowship (BSF).

Cecilia was a seasoned believer in Bible study but BSF would be my first. I had never studied the Bible in a small-group setting along with women I had just met. What if I couldn't answer a question? Would they laugh at me or think I was dumb? Thankfully, I tried it. I sat and listened. No one made me answer anything. I left that first night wanting to know more—so much more.

As we met each Monday night, I fell in love with my Bible as I began to understand its meanings. I learned so much that I completed all five years of the course. BSF is a great way to learn your Bible. It is international, so look it up and see if it in your area (www.BSFInternational.org). I highly recommend it.

As I grew in knowledge of truth, I became captivated by God and His love for me. I desired Him. I wanted what Cecilia had and what my brother and sister-in-law had. As Rob and I sat in the hot tub at our apartment complex, I shared with Rob all that I was learning. While I was growing, he had become uninterested, and he stopped attending church with me. I faced dissolving expectations of what I had wanted marriage to be. We weren't connecting like I thought we would. I felt so alone and helpless in this foreign land with a disinterested husband.

I attended church alone. This wasn't how I envisioned it, but God remained faithful, and He walked with me. God also gave me another Timothy to help me along in my walk. Both Candace and Cecilia walked with me as I navigated a marriage where I was growing in my faith without my husband. While Candace and her husband worked with Rob, God gave me hope that Rob would come to believe. "Wait, Carol. Love Rob into the faith," was God's sweet voice to my soul. He helped me to understand that Rob working seven days a week was a disguise. Rob was hiding from me. God gave me hope that eventually He would bring us together spiritually.

The Woes of Waiting

When God speaks, you can be sure that it will come to pass. This is such a comfort to know that you can trust His Word. The hard part is the waiting. And waiting makes you ponder and wonder and, unfortunately, doubt what He has told you. We like to help God out and move forward in our own thinking.

Abram's wife, Sarai, had trouble with waiting. Abram is the same as Abraham. God renamed him at the age of ninety-nine! God changed Sarai to Sarah at the age of ninety.[1] Abraham was going to become the father of a multitude of nations.[2] But how, when they were past childbearing years?

Never underestimate the power of God!

God spoke to Abraham, telling him that he will have an heir of his own, a son. Abraham shared the message with his wife. This must have felt like nonsense to her. Sarah might have had the same reaction I would have had, rolling my eyes in disbelief with a sarcastic comment. Even though Sarah was beyond childbearing years, she still dreamed of having a child of her own. In the long, dark days of waiting and wondering, Sarah couldn't wait on God anymore. It was time to take matters into her own hands.

She concocted a way for them to have a baby. "Hey, Abraham, go sleep with my servant and get her pregnant so I can have a child!"[3] Seriously, are her and I any different? I wouldn't wait for Rob to become a believer before marrying him, and Sarah couldn't wait any longer either! Waiting causes laziness in your faith walk. It causes you to believe that God does not see you or hear you. You take the reins of control from God and tell Him that you can do a better job. Again, you take a bite from Eve's apple. Are you keeping track of all the bite marks you make? Yet, God still loves you.

My waiting time for Rob to become a believer could have been lengthy. I would hear stories of people waiting decades for loved ones to see Christ. You may have someone in your life that you are waiting for. Don't stop praying and believing, no matter the length of time. We are each in God's hands, and He calls us individually.

God Hears My Heart

I had made a commitment to God and to Rob when I said, "I do." Despite our rocky start of being unequally yoked, I waited, believed, and trusted God. We reached that time in our relationship when we were ready to start a family. I was apprehensive about Rob not being a believer, but my two friends told me to give it to God and let Him do what He needs to do. Five years and eighty-eight days later, my prayer for my husband came true. Our son Alex was born, and Rob saw God.

The blood of Jesus erases your bite marks and makes you whole.

Before Alex's birth, Rob had told me that the only way he could believe God was for God to come and sit down next to him and prove Himself. The morning after Alex's birth, Rob lay in the hospital bed with me as we stared at our son in his bassinet. Rob told me that he was going to start coming to church with me. When I asked him what changed, he pointed to Alex, "There is a God when you watch your wife give birth to your son." I became Wonder Woman to my husband. Not to brag, but he still sees me this way.

I am so thankful that God is bigger than any excuses we can make. God is faithful and committed. He heard my cries. He knew my desires and He saw me. God was deepening my faith foundation all the more. I was learning to trust and believe when He spoke to me. Two and a half years later, God blessed us with our daughter, Katie.

Rob saw God through his son, and through his daughter, God was going to teach him how to trust Him. I remembered having a dream while pregnant with Katie in which God had revealed that she was a girl, what she looked like, and that I was nursing her. When she was born, she looked exactly the same as in my dream. I was very thankful for that dream because I had struggled with nursing, and I had gotten anxious over it. God gave me that precursor so that I could know and believe that everything would be alright. I did nurse her, and God tenderly spoke to my soul, "I will always prepare you, Carol. I am with you. I hear your heart for I care for you." *And God has never let me down.*

God's Love Softens Differences

The first five years of our marriage were arduous for the both of us. When two people come together to share life, there are always good times and frustrating times. I can't say bad times because we haven't had bad times, just a lot of frustrating times. We are both introverted, so we don't mind alone time. We both agree financially, so money has never been a struggle. We like simple things, which makes life easier. It doesn't take much to entertain ourselves.

Then there are the opposites: he likes the outdoors, while I like being indoors; he likes hot weather, while I like it colder; he is a busybody, whereas I like to chill out; he has an engineering mindset, and I am creative and visual; he remains calm and level-headed, and I get anxious and uptight. Shall I add that we communicate differently? Very differently. I process with compassion and feel things very deeply and personally. Rob, on the other hand, processes mechanically and sees situations as problems that need fixing. Once fixed, you move on. Mix all this in with selfishness and expectations and you get yourself some arduous chaos. Yes, chaos that could have ended our marriage many times throughout our years.

It still could, if we focus on Eve's apple. God reassured me that even when only one spouse believes and is learning to follow after

God, He blesses and honors the union. I am in awe over God and His love for us. Many times, in our thirty-plus years, we both didn't know what to do, with each other and with ourselves. God always made a way for us to come together, every time.

God makes a way when you don't think there is a way.

God recently cleared away a gigantic roadblock in our relationship. After three decades of waiting, I had lost hope. I had conceded that life was as good as it was going to get. I want you to understand that I married a wonderful man. He has gone above and beyond to provide for his family. He works hard and keeps his promises. He has given me a great life. So, you may be asking: what was the problem? While Rob was great at focusing on tangible things, things he had control over, he lacked in connecting with me emotionally.

He would listen when I talked, but if he couldn't fix it, he moved on and left me to learn how to deal with my issues on my own. This left me feeling lonely. During these trying times, God would meet me in my loneliness and be the void that Rob couldn't fill. *God is like that, you know. He fills those empty spaces with Himself.* People will fall short. I will fail to meet someone's needs, and so will you. We are not made to be perfect. We are made to let God complete us and, in turn, show us how to love others.

From the summer of 2019 through March 2020, Rob and I struggled greatly because we were both entering the empty-nest season. The kids had been a buffer for us for many years, but then we went back to being just the two of us. Alex was settling into married life and Katie had left for an employment adventure with Disney in Orlando. You could say that I grieved deeply the mothering season that God had graciously allowed me to have. Amidst the grief, God called me to start a ministry, United in Love, and to grow a platform so this book can get published. God wanted me to move forward. "Carol, I have something new for you."

Letting go of my favorite season to begin another one—one that has taken me completely out of my comfort zone—has caused me much angst. Like I mentioned before, I do not do well with change. I struggled and, as usual, Rob did not meet me in the middle. He wasn't taking the time to understand what I was going through. Although I felt alone, God never left my side. He meets me, sees me, hears me, and helps me. Jesus fills the voids left by others.

I understood that God can change hearts. He is the heart transplant doctor. Rob and I are both amazed and humbled over how much we have changed through the years. We give all the credit to God for being so committed to us and always making a way for our marriage to endure. However, free will stood in the way. I knew that God could work in Rob, but what if Rob didn't want to see? I would question what I wasn't understanding. What was missing between us? Why were we not coming together? There has always been a wedge of something that remained between the two of us. I was done asking these same questions I have asked for the last twenty-five years. Then God showed up, like He always does when His timing is right.

Rob was willing to read a godly marriage book with me. I asked him to find one and he did. As we sat together, Rob read the text, and I read the scripture references. We would then talk about what we had read. What it evolved into was us talking our problems out, getting real with each other—and Rob was owning his side of things. And what do you know? God showed up big time. I mean, like, holy cow, God, this was huge. You are amazing!

I had to wait for Rob to be ready to see. God had taught me how to meet in the middle, but it took Rob longer. God woke Rob up and now, after a couple months of reading and praying (we are almost done with our second book), I am not alone anymore. *Rob not only hears me, but he sees me.* After thirty-one years of marriage, God cleared the roadblock, that wedge that hindered our relationship from coming together.

I can't explain how He has been the constant anchor for us, but He has. He straightens our path so we can walk together. Only God can do that. I hope this inspires you to keep looking up. Waiting on God is worth it—it's not easy, but it is worth it. You will have to humble yourself and be patient. The enemy will do everything to distract and divide, but God will see you through when you persist and persevere.

I want you to know that God has not dropped you off on the roadside and left you for dead in any relationship. Whatever situation you are facing, God has not left your side and He is fighting behind the scenes for you and your partner. Believe and do not give up! Fight for your marriage. Fight for your wayward child. Fight for that friendship. Fight for your faith. Fight, for your life depends on it, and when you fight, you learn to follow Him and not yourself. He has a process of helping you to let go of yourself and become more like Jesus so that you can go and be His light in this dark world.

Finish Strong in Your Faith Walk

Rob has taught the kids and me this motto: "Finish strong." Whenever you begin something, you see the task through until it is completed. This was one of Rob's strengths that drew me to him. He persevered and would continue working at something even if it was difficult.

Jesus persevered on this earth for thirty-three years and completed what God had called Him to do so that you and I can be redeemed. Rob taught our children to persevere and finish strong with whatever they had to do, whether school or activities. I would encourage perseverance in their friendships and their walks with God. *With God, how you finish is more important than how you started.* 2 Timothy 4:7 says, "I have fought the good fight. I have finished the race, and I have remained faithful."

This mentality has helped Rob and me to thrive in our marriage. We view our relationship in the light of who God is and how He loves us. This is our foundation for how we treat each other, our children, and everyone else. We love each other in our strengths and weaknesses. This love embraces acceptance and patience.

We laugh over how we are like sandpaper to one another. We laugh over how if we divorced and found other partners, we would then irritate them. We might as well irritate each other so we don't drive anybody else nuts. Amidst our struggles, we have learned how to laugh. Life can get pretty heavy and dark quickly. God is gracious in how He created laughter. It lightens the mood, and it helps place us in the right perspective.

As I have gone public with my faith and started a blog and Bible study website, Satan has been ruthless. He does not want this book to be published and for United in Love to prosper. He likes to disrupt the unity that is between Rob and me. You see,

You have that one thing that is a thorn in your side.

marital stress has always been the enemy's tactic when he wants to subdue me. It is like a thorn in my side. I don't know why, but I have had to learn to recognize this and hunker down with God and His Word. God has been faithful for thirty-plus years and He will continue to until He takes one of us home.

You have to see the truth of who you are in your sinful earthly condition before God's healing love can penetrate and heal you. In this life, one needs a sense of humor and an openness to change or else sin will divide and conquer, giving Satan the satisfaction.

Thank goodness God walks with me and gives me discernment as I continue to grow in Him. I have learned like Peter in John 6:68: "Lord, to whom would we go? You have the words that give eternal life." God is all I have to count on, depend on, and trust. I confidently know that I can rest assured that God has His hand on my marriage, my kids, this ministry and book, my health, and my all.

Chapter Eight

A Heart Transplant

"And I will give you a new heart,
and I will put a new spirit in you. I will take your
stony, stubborn heart and give you a
tender, responsive heart."
— *Ezekiel 36:26*

In the midst of our early years of chaos, God gave me many scriptures that I could hold onto while God was working in Rob's heart. Even though two become one in the sight of God, we each grow independently. As we each mature in faith, God is the one who brings unity to the marriage union. What brings about discord is the reality that neither party can make their spouse mature in the same way and at the same time. Thus, there may be waiting times, lots of them, and a need for patience.

In the introduction of this book when I referenced Isaiah 41:10, I shared one of the earliest times when God helped me to see how real He is. Jesus making His presence known changes you. My heart grew in a way that altered how I view things. I mentioned being out of sync with Rob. The constant battle of never meeting in the middle is emotionally draining. I hope you don't mind, but I want to share more about how God spoke to me on the couch that day.

As I read Isaiah 41:10, "Fear not, Carol, for I am with you"—I want to stop right here for a minute. I have added my name for a reason. I want you to understand that the Bible is God's personal love letter to you. If you were the only person on earth, Jesus would come and die for you so that you could have a relationship with God and share life together. Did you know that when Jesus was on the cross, you (insert your name) were on His mind? I believe there is a song about that.

Back to the verse: "Fear not, Carol, for I am with you. Do not be dismayed for I am your God. I will strengthen you. I will help you. I will uphold you with my victorious right hand." In this defining moment in my faith, God was telling me that He knew my circumstances and that He was working on my behalf. He is still committed to me, and my friends, He knows your circumstances, and He is committed to you.

He will meet you right where you are, in the midst of rebelling against Him. Rebelling might be a harsh word, but it is what it is. When you are making your own decisions in your own way for your own life, you live in rebellion against who you are made to be. Remember, you are part of Adam and Eve's legacy. You cannot remove yourself from their lineage. *You either look to God, or you keep eating apples.*

God was changing me to become His servant. He led me and taught me with a gentle hand, a hand that held mine and took me forward, baby-step by baby-step, in a consistent and loving manner. He prodded me ahead in ways that I could understand. He increased my heart's desire to want to know Him, and it all began with studying scripture. 2 Timothy 3:16 says that "All Scripture is inspired by God and is useful to teach us what is true and to make us realize what is wrong in our lives. It corrects us when we are wrong and teaches us to do what is right." God uses marriage to teach me about Him and to love unconditionally.

God Was Creating a New Me

I love Cinderella, the whole princess and Prince Charming story and living happily ever after. I came into marriage with similar expectations. Rob was my Prince Charming and he was going to sweep me off my feet all the time. I had expectations that Rob was not meeting, and I felt cheated and angry when he didn't meet them. He had to tell me that I had him on a high pedestal and that he could never meet my expectations. I needed to hear that. I kept fumbling as I handled married life with my expectations of perfection with a short-fuse. Adding a new career along with living in a new part of the country made our chaos all the more entertaining, to say the least.

God will use what He deems necessary to help you to see Him.

As I look back, I am amazed and in awe over how God has taken a shy, insecure, stubborn young girl who gets mad easily and has molded her into a secure, strong, and calmer woman. While many seek answers to their problems in a variety of ways, there is one way which deals with the root causes of our issues. The root lies deep within the heart. I needed a new heart, and God gave me one when I called on Him. Ezekiel 36:26 says, "And I will give you a new heart, and I will put a new spirit in you. I will take out your stony, stubborn heart and give you a tender, responsive heart." God promises to never leave your side as He refills you with Himself.

My part of the process involved a "heart transplant" and a rewiring of my mindset in how I saw God, myself, and others. I had a great deal of inner turmoil that erupted on those who were closest to me. Anxiety brought out my anger and impatience. Unhealthy expectations can do a great deal of damage. I am ever so thankful for having the perfect Teacher. He had a personal plan to help me learn and grow. He met me in my circumstances, and He came to me in a way that He could get my attention.

Welcome to the Quietness of the Night

Amidst the busyness of motherhood and tending to a home, I was not very disciplined in my time spent with God and His Word. Sometimes I took the time and sometimes I didn't. I lived by my feelings and the circumstances that surrounded me. Since I was so irregular in spending time with God, He would wake me up in the middle of the night. At first, I would be annoyed and lie there thinking of this and that until I realized that God was speaking pertinent things to me. However, by morning I would not retain what He had told me.

Eventually, I would write down what He said, and to my surprise, journaling my thoughts has developed into a love for writing. My dates with God eventually became more regular. My soul became fed. He didn't wake me every night, but often enough, He spoke tenderly to my tumultuous soul and began to reveal Himself. I fell in love with our date nights and God Himself. He faithfully gave me strength to endure my busy days.

Have you noticed God speaking to you? He will speak to you in ways that you will recognize. The question is: do you want to hear? It is easy to get so preoccupied with life that you become oblivious to His presence. You see Him when you want to or when you feel you need Him. You respond to yourself first, and then you seek Him when you are out of other options. I did that. It took marriage and living in a "foreign" land to get me to look up at Him. To my surprise, God was ready and waiting.

Into the Dressing Room We Go

Change is not easy for many people. Allowing God to change you is humbling, hard, and uncomfortable. I liken it to trying on new clothes. I feel out of place when I try on a new style. I like familiarity and comfort. New shoes are the same way. There is this transition time with new clothes and shoes. In the dressing room, they fit nice, but once you get them home and actually wear them, they either become favorites or they end up in the back of the closet until rummage sale time. You don't know until you wear them.

God wants you to get a new wardrobe and be clothed with items that will enhance your beauty in Him. God wants you to be comfortable in His attire. But you have to get in the fitting room and try truth on. It might not feel comfortable at first, but eventually you will find that God's style fits you like a glove, like Jesus jeggings.

As you grow accustomed to being in His Word, you will want to wear nothing else. Trust me on this. You won't have a tummy pooching out or a saggy behind. The only muffin top that will be seen is on your plate for breakfast. Isaiah 61:10 says, "I am overwhelmed with joy in the LORD my God! For He has dressed me with the clothing of salvation and draped me in a robe of righteousness. I am like a bridegroom in his wedding suit or a bride

God is ready for you to meet Him in the most wonderful ways.

with her jewels." Galatians 3:27 says, "And all who have been united with Christ in baptism have put on Christ, like putting on new clothes."

We like God to change and conform to our needs and wishes, don't we? But this is not reality. God is God and we are made to become holy like His Son. It is not the other way around. *We are to let God take us into His fitting room and let Him style us to fit His plan.*

You have a role to play in the span of time that He has you on earth, and you need to be fitted appropriately. God takes His apparel and conforms it to you in a way that you will feel your best. You will be able to walk down the street with your head held high and a kick in your step. He fills your heart with goodness and love, and your mindset has had a makeover. This is when you have joy in your heart and your soul is alive. You are a sight of beauty to God as you live for Him. I like to sing songs as I go about my day. I am out of key, but God doesn't care because my joy comes from Him and it is all for Him.

In God's fitting room, you will find Romans 12:2 posted on the wall: "Don't copy the behavior and customs of this world, but let God transform you into a new person by changing the way you think. Then you will learn to know God's will for you, which is good and pleasing and per-

Look in the mirror and say this: I am beautiful to God.

fect." He gives you a new path to take, one that is better than any path that the world has to offer.

God Hears My Desires

As I sought God and learned from Him, I found that He was not only answering my prayers, He was answering my heart's desires that I was aware of, and even ones that I didn't realize. I desired to get a college degree. God honored that. I desired to be married and to stay home and have children. God honored that.

Then there are those quiet inner desires that no one knows about except God and me. This is where God has astonished me with his commitment to helping me change—in my marriage, for my children, and with other relationships. He began with changing my heart first.

I desired reprieve from my anger. Remember how I shared that I have a headstrong mindset? Anger likes to hang around and stir itself up whenever it wants. I remember telling God that I know He is very capable of removing the angst that is within me. I felt confident that freedom is coming. I believed. God answered me, but not in the way I wanted. "Yes, I can remove it from you, Carol, but I want you to let me control it in you instead." Ugh. Didn't God know my way would have been easier for me? God was teaching me that my life was not about me. I was to learn that my role was to trust, obey, and concede to God's will. This has been a forty-year process, and I know it will continue until He takes me home.

Along with scripture, three books have helped me greatly in gaining freedom with my headstrong mindset. One is *It's Not About Me* by Max Lucado. Another one is *Battlefield of the Mind* by Joyce Meyers, and the third book is one I just read called, *Get Out of Your Head* by Jennie Allen. These books were game changers for me in my faith walk.

Our troubles start in our heads with our thoughts, and the enemy knows it. He perches himself on our shoulders, and he whispers sweet nothings into our ears, just like he did with Eve and Adam. We are called to stop the bad thoughts from taking root and growing. We are to destroy rebellious thoughts at the foot of the cross. We are to hold every thought captive.[1]

He reminds me of what is of utmost importance, which is His presence. He is with me always. This has nothing to do with how He chooses to answer my prayers or fix any of my problems. Whether I am relieved of something or not, God's presence is all that matters. He is all I need, and He is all you need.

I try to live life so that I'm not holding on to anything so tightly that the stars in my eyes are dictating my decisions. I made a vow to God that I would never box Him in again to suit my needs and wants, like I did when Rob and I were engaged.

His presence is what you are seeking, what you are after.

I have seen many lives that were full of struggles and regret all because they held on too tightly to an earthly thing. Even if it is your heart's most desired dream, you are to lay everything at the foot of the cross. Let God use you as He sees fit. He will help you to let go of your most precious wants and replace them with more beautiful blessings. Peace is what you will experience along with joy and contentment.

Many things are probably going through your mind right now like doubt, apprehension, and perhaps fear. The devil does not want you to realize reality. He wants to keep you locked in your doubts, fears, insecurities, and whatever else is keeping you chained up. The devil does not want you to realize the beauty and potential that lies within you. He loves it when you look in the mirror and see inadequacy instead of greatness, ugliness instead of beauty. You have been deceived, my friend, for way too long. Who's with me in ending the lies of our defeated foe? Read that again, *our defeated foe.*

God Wants to Dance with You

The way I would describe my relationship with God in the early years was a dance. My parents loved to dance. Knowing how to do the waltz, they would glide around the dance floor. God and I would try the waltz, but it was not as smooth as my parents. God led, and I kept kicking him in the knees and stepping on His feet. I wasn't conceding to His will and way. Instead, I wanted God to go my way and dance the way I thought the waltz should be. Thank goodness He has had patience with me. He has never let go of my hand nor removed His arm from around me. He simply continues to pursue me, love me, and accept me. He sees me. He has convinced me of His love as He continues to show me that He is the better way.

God honors what you hold dear. God cares what concerns you. When you choose God to lead, you put yourself under His umbrella of protection and you put yourself into a bigger field to roam around in, with greater opportunities to experience. God takes what you have to offer and transforms it.

Like I shared before, there were times in our marriage where Rob and I wondered what should we do next? We weren't seeing eye to eye, and there didn't seem to be a solution. God is committed to marriages and everything else. He was always able to bring both of us to a new place of love, forgiveness, and understanding. God opened up opportunities for Rob and me to discover how He elevated our relationship to a place of greater love. All we had to do was to ask Him to make a way. This has amazed and humbled the both of us.

God's Unveiling His Love

You need to realize that you have blinders over your eyes and ears. You need the unveiling of Christ's redeeming love and His truth to remove your rebellious tendencies so you can become more like Him. 2 Corinthians 4:3-5 says, "If the Good News we preach (through our words and actions) is hidden behind a veil, it is hidden only from people who are perishing. Satan, who is the god of this world, has blinded the minds of those who don't believe. They are unable to see the glorious light of the Good News. They don't understand this message about the glory of Christ, who is the exact likeness of God. You see, we don't go around preaching about ourselves. We preach that Jesus Christ is Lord and we ourselves are your servants for Jesus's sake."

Because of our lineage with Adam and Eve, we must make our way to the hope that can redeem us back to God. 2 Corinthians 3:18 explains what happens when we let Jesus penetrate our heart and mind: "So, all of us who have had that veil removed can see and reflect the glory of the Lord. And the Lord, who is the Spirit, makes us more and more like Him as we are changed into His glorious image." Beauty transpires and lives become whole when Jesus gets involved.

I had the privilege of watching my mother change more fully into His image. She always believed in God. She loved singing in the church choir, mothering her eight children, and working alongside my dad in the co-op store. She stretched her dollars to serve her family. She married her Prince Charming, and they were blessed with forty-six years of marriage. She would talk about having disappointments and sorrows along her path as well as all the good times.

At a time when she wasn't ready for it, God came for her Prince Charming. My father was her life. He was seventy-four and she was sixty-nine. For eighteen months after he passed, she was very angry with God as to why God would take him. They were supposed to enjoy retirement but couldn't because he had been sick for nine years with heart issues. She cared for him so faithfully while he had to live in a nursing home in his final years. They exhibited committed love. Although God ended their marriage, He continued to faithfully care for my mother in her last ten years of life.

While my mom believed in God, my father was her number one man. She had counted on him for everything—more than God. She even went to church because of him. Knowing this, I wonder if I would have reacted the same way as my mother if Rob had met all my needs? Would I have looked to Rob more than God? I have become thankful for my marriage to Rob, even amidst hardships. I have fallen in love with the Lover of my soul and in return He has given me a believing husband, children who walk with God, unity, peace, laughter, and most importantly, God Himself.

Losing her best friend was crushing to my mom. As I would listen to her vent her feelings, I would gently guide her to go to God, even in her anger. "He can handle your anger, Mom," I would tell her. She struggled with talking so openly to God. I would reassure her that He would help her through her hurt and anger. She focused on what they hadn't gotten to experience, like retirement. I helped her to recollect all the things that God had blessed her and Dad with. God did honor and answer many of their desires through the course of their marriage.

God loved my mom, even in her seventies. He would fill the voids that made her life feel empty and alone. He can do that, you know. He meets you and fills you up with Himself. Because of sin, we all struggle with loneliness, insecurities, and feeling needy, but God, in His infinite love, comes and rescues us from these three foes that plague us. God loves His children faithfully and completely.

Age is not a factor for God. He will reveal Himself to any open heart at any age. My mom had the opportunity to go on an Emmaus Walk, which is a seventy-two-hour spiritual renewal retreat. I loved her response to me when she returned. "Carol, your mother has gotten her head screwed on straight." What she meant was that she had finally taken a step of faith beyond just believing, and she now had a relationship with Jesus Christ. Jesus became her husband and she His bride.

She began reading and studying her Bible. God even brought a man named Norman into her life. They had both lost their spouses. She was like a little schoolgirl crushing on a cute boy. She would get flustered when he came around. It was the cutest thing to watch. God cared enough to tend to my mother's needs. It was comforting for me to watch God fill up her soul.

Norman and Mom began hosting a Bible study in her apartment. She would have never done something like that in her earlier years. She led the worship part. She had a beautiful alto voice and would sing duets. In her new relationship with a Man that stole her heart (and I don't mean Norman), God wooed her to a deeper calling, and she embraced it. Oh, how God's love is timeless. No one is so set in his ways that he cannot change when God gets involved.

God receives people of all ages.

Can you imagine what families, neighborhoods, cities, states, and our country would look like if people would simply take their eyes off themselves and live out God's Word? I truly believe that we would see fewer shooting rampages, less segregation, less protesting, and more intimate communities and neighborhoods. I believe there would be less corruption and more resources available for everyone. There wouldn't be homelessness and hunger.

Although God pursues people to come to Him every day, we convince ourselves that we don't need to change. *If only we would give obedience a chance.* Unfortunately, we let this word, *obedience*, stop us. We envision living like a monk or a nun sitting around praying and reading scripture all day. While God has called some to a strict celibate lifestyle, He wants to lead you to where obedience causes fulfillment, peace, strength, and an organized mindset to unfold within you. Life gets exciting when you get on the tandem bike and God is in front.

Here are other bonuses to living with God: he extends your hours, your thoughts are more orderly, and you get more done in less time. That's because God is the God of order. He was orderly when He created everything, and you are to be orderly in your life and when you worship. 1 Corinthians 14:33 and verse 40 says, "For God is not a God of disorder but of peace, as in all the meetings of God's holy people. But be sure that everything is done properly and in order." You need to let God change you so that you can reflect Jesus in your life, no matter what age you are.

Chapter Nine

GOD IS FOR YOU

"Don't be afraid, for I am with you.
Don't be discouraged, for I am your God.
I will strengthen you and help you. I will
hold you up with my victorious right hand."
— Isaiah 41:10

G od is for you. It is that plain and simple. But as mentioned earlier, our adversary threw a curve ball at the first couple, Adam and Eve, and we have been in a downward spiral since. Until Jesus returns, earth will continue to decay. Consider the virus that has infected the whole world recently. It isn't the first one, and it won't be the last. Consider all the political upheaval, injustices with race and our law enforcement, and the organized riots that are infiltrating American cities. When you study history, you see these same issues erupting time and time again. It's all because of the Fall in the Garden, and it will continue until Jesus returns to make things right.

Throughout these chapters, I continually bring up Satan and how he is messing things up. I have done this on purpose because we easily forget. We won't embrace who God is unless we understand how sinful we are. It's like being an alcoholic. No help will avail until you confess that you have a problem. We need to see the deep pit that God has to pull us out of in order to save us. It is a deep, dirty, stinky, and mucky pit that only Jesus's blood can redeem us from.

The Great "I Am"

The great "I Am" provides a way for you to live above your unrefined existence until He restores His creation to how it was intended to be in the first place. In the present moment, God is here for you. You are never alone. God is loving you, battling for you, and helping you to enjoy the life that He has given you. When God talks in present tense, He is speaking of His eternal existence.

Throughout the Bible, He references Himself in a way that lets you know that He is in this very moment. Revelation 1:8 says, "'I AM the Alpha and the Omega, the Beginning and the End,' says the Lord God. 'I AM the one who is, who always was, and who is still to come—the Almighty One.'" As you read scripture, be on the lookout for how God refers to Himself and how He expects man to respond.

A great verse is John 15:5, in which Jesus speaks, "Yes, I AM the vine; you are the branches. Those who remain in me, and I in them, will produce much fruit. For apart from me you can do nothing." Jesus is speaking in present tense, and He gives you directions in how to live. What you learn is that your life will be fruitful when you walk with Christ and that you are incapable of achieving anything meaningful without Him. You may be successful in worldly ways, but those are for a short season. God's ways are eternal and everlasting.

God Pursues Despite Our Sin

God speaks in various ways that you can understand when your heart and mind are watchful for Him. He is unwavering in His pursuit of His children. For many, this may be an irritant. Our human nature likes to do what it wants to do and dislikes being corrected.

What are natural responses to correction? Anger is a common one. Embarrassment and wanting to hide are ones I deal with. The blame game is a fan favorite. Let's travel back to Adam and Eve in the Garden. When you reread Genesis 3, God reveals how man's character responds when backed into a corner.

Adam and Eve heard God walking around in the Garden, so they hid. This was the first time that they did that. God called for Adam who then told God that he hid and was afraid because he was naked. Even though God knew that they had eaten from the forbidden tree, he allowed them to admit their wrongdoings. You see how blame reared its ugly head as Adam blamed Eve, and Eve blamed the serpent.

You are getting a good picture of how sin wrecks life. Disobedience brings on a multitude of problems that cause disruption after disruption in relationships. You masquerade with fear and shame and if needed, you blame others. It has been this way since the beginning of time. God is not taken aback or surprised, and He faithfully continues to pursue you to look up at Him.

As you read in the rest of Genesis 3, God disciplined each of them. Life became how we know it today, toilsome, with struggles and joy mixed in. Before He banished them from the Garden, he clothed and cared for them. This has not changed. He makes His presence known to each person.

I love hearing people's testimonies of how they came to believe and trust Jesus. Each story has a common denominator. They lived in opposition to God and knew it, and they came to a realization that they were meant for more than their life on earth. Even people who are living successfully by worldly standards find that all the pleasures of this earth still don't satisfy the heart. Something is missing, and contentment is always beyond their reach.

Read the book of Ecclesiastes. Solomon had everything that life could offer, and he found that it all was futile and meaningless. That is because this earth was not his home, and it isn't yours either. You are simply traveling through without knowing how long you will be here. Life on earth is preparation for living in His presence. This side of the journey is where man decides for himself what his forever tomorrow will be, either heaven with God or separation from God.

When Adam spoke truthfully to God, he was revealing the secret of how you need to live. When God was looking for him, he could have stayed hidden and not answered. We do that, don't we? It has become very apparent in society today. More and more people are not caring who God is. I never thought I would see the day that life has no value anymore in the United States. Comfort and ease has deafened and blinded Americans. You are to respond like Adam. When God calls, even when you are in the wrong, you are to answer Him and talk honestly and openly.

God Loves the *Wheel of Fortune* Game

God is present in your life and He makes Himself accessible in intimate ways. One way is through prayer. Because of Jesus, you can approach His throne boldly and receive mercy and grace.[1] Adam talking with God in the Garden is a perfect example of prayer: simple, honest and real. God wants nothing more than for you to come to Him for all your needs. Unfortunately, you get so distracted by your own desires that you neglect this gift that you so desperately need to open and capitalize on.

In the tenth chapter of Luke, you read about two sisters. One knows what is important and the other gets easily distracted. Mary is at Jesus's feet while Martha is busy fussing in the kitchen. I am a Martha more than a Mary, which means I get distracted with chores like

Martha. My eyes focus on tending to my home and the needs of my family before talking with God.

It is good to know that God desires intimacy. He uses the very things that distract you to get you to stop and look up. On one particular day, God used a trivial moment to reveal to me how He desires to converse with me moment by moment.

Back when handheld games were popular, I had the *Wheel of Fortune* game. It was fun to see how high a score I could get. When Mom would visit, she played my game, so for Christmas, we gave her one. I happened to obtain a very high score, and I thought I may have reached my limit. Mom was impressed by how high a score I had received, and she felt she would never achieve that level. Oh, what fun we can have over the simplest of things. They are bonding moments that are hand-delivered by God Himself.

When Mom returned home, she would call me and tell me how high a score she had reached. We enjoyed encouraging each other. Then one day she called and said that *she had beaten my high score.* I couldn't believe it, nor could she. We laughed about it and shared a great memory together.

Let's pause for a moment. We all would agree that this bantering about scores is fun and trivial, but it turned into so much more. After hanging up, I went about my day and wondered whether it was possible to get a higher score. I stopped what I was doing and sat down and played a round to see if I could really beat her new high score. As I was playing, I thought to myself, "I should pray about getting a higher score." I pondered that for a moment but quickly rationalized, "Carol, don't be so silly. God wouldn't answer a prayer like that. It's just a game."

Silly me for downplaying our Sovereign God. God used an ordinary, simple moment and changed my thinking. I played a round, and you guessed it, I beat Mom's score. I couldn't believe that. God had heard me. I felt a nudge in my spirit, "See." Of course, I had to call Mom and tell her, and once again we both laughed.

Amidst bonding moments, you have a God that hears and sees you. He uses all things to lead you to a place where you will know without a shadow of a doubt that He is with you. God met me one afternoon to show me who He is in a moment of daily, ordinary living. Something changes within you when you know that the hand of God is upon you, just like the time in my family room when Jesus leaned over my shoulder to read Isaiah 41:10 to me. My spirit stood a little taller that day as God elevated my trust level in Him.

God is awakening you to His Presence.

Little did I know that God had built an altar in my heart. He does that, you know. He reveals Himself in ways that will change you from the inside out. *He builds these little altars so that you remember and know that His love is upon you.* He reassures you that you are never alone. All these little moments become bricks that lay your faith foundation, and you become stronger and stronger in Him.

Prayer Is as Simple as Saying Hello

As altars are being erected in your heart, and as your faith starts to bloom, you become more aware of God's presence. This awareness causes you to seek Him all the more, and you search wholeheartedly for what your soul is needing. You not only receive His presence but are able to converse with Him personally. Your soul is intertwined with the Holy Spirit to the point where you can communicate with God. *This is known as prayer.*

There is a well-known prayer that is used often, the Lord's Prayer. Many churches recite this prayer every Sunday. Reciting things repeatedly causes you to miss out on the personal experience you get when you are engaged with the Father. You get so comfortable with head knowledge that you cease to reach out to God Himself. Do you know that God gave this particular prayer as a guide in how to talk to Him? In Matthew 6, you see Jesus telling His disciples to "pray like this."

In Matthew 6:7-8, Jesus tells people, "Don't babble on and on as people of other religions do. They think their prayers are answered merely by repeating their words again and again." Jesus says not to do that. You are to believe that God knows what you need and trust that He hears you. Prayer is to be intimate, honest, and personal. The Holy Spirit needs to lead you in your prayers, or else your petitions become about you.

While writing this book, the pastor of my church gave a sermon on how to use the Lord's Prayer as a guide in talking with God. Based off of Pastor Matt Claussen's sermon, here is what you can learn. "This is a prayer that is not to be used solely for repetition. While repetition helps in remembering things, it is an outline to use which focuses on who God is and how you should respond." By praying this way, you learn how to engage with God in a personal way. The pastor broke down the prayer into six parts:

PART 1: *"Our Father in heaven, hallowed be Thy name"* – You have the honor and privilege to be in the presence of the Almighty Father. He walks with you, even when you have wandered away. It is unfortunate that your mind can't fully grasp how close He is, otherwise your posture toward God would be totally different.

You are to hallow His name. What does this mean? The name of God is sacred, holy, anointed, and divine. He is the highest of the highest. There is no one above Him. When you commune with God, you are reaching beyond the stars, not just for them. You can liken the name of God to winning the gold medal in the Olympics. For an athlete, there is no higher award to achieve.

You begin talking with God by aligning yourself with a humbled heart on bent knees. You are to praise Him for who He is and what He has done in your life. You are to exalt His name. "I will exalt you, my God and King, and praise your name forever and ever. I will praise you every day; yes, I will praise you forever. Great is the LORD! He is most worthy of praise! No one can measure His greatness."[2]

PART 2: *"Thy Kingdom come"* – Jesus is returning. As each day passes, you get closer and closer to that glorious day. God's creation has been in flux since Adam and Eve left the Garden. Sin has turned the world upside down. Since then, much time has passed, and man has achieved great discoveries and inventions that have caused us to shift our eyes off of God. We have lost sight of who we are in comparison to Him. We have forgotten that God is the one who gave the wisdom and insight for things to be discovered. We have elevated ourselves to being our own gods. We need to return God to His rightful place.

As you wait for His return, you are to pray for the salvation of those around you who need Jesus and for your own salvation. You need Jesus to reign in your life. Remember, He bridges the gap between God and man. "So also, Christ died once for all time as a sacrifice to take away the sins of many people.

He will come again, not to deal with our sins, but to bring salvation to all who are eagerly waiting for Him."[3]

PART 3: *"Thy will be done, on earth as it is in Heaven"* – Ask God to help with accepting His will. His plan has been carried out since the beginning of time, and it will continue to move forward whether you align yourself to Him or not. It is good to remember what God says, for He trumps our own free will. "Jesus came and told His disciples, 'I have been given all authority in heaven and on earth.'"[4]

PART 4: *"Give us this day our daily bread"* – You are to pray for your necessities. You are not to get caught up in asking for things that are beyond what you need. In the United States, most of us have more than we need. It is easy to lose our focus in abundance. I believe living through the COVID-19 pandemic is helping many people to get reacquainted with what is important: the simple things in life. "Look at the birds. They don't plant or harvest or store food in barns, for your Heavenly Father feeds them. And aren't you far more valuable to Him than they are?"[5]

PART 5: *"And forgive us our trespasses, as we forgive those who have trespassed against us"* – You are to examine yourself and confess any sins. This is not about focusing on others' faults and praying for them. You are to focus on God and His amazing mercy towards you as you ask for forgiveness. "But if we confess our sins to Him, He is faithful and just to forgive us our sins and to cleanse us from all wickedness."[6] God is capable of healing you from your sins.

PART 6: *"And lead us not into temptation but deliver us from evil"* – Pray for God's protection from temptation and sin. Evil is everywhere, and it never takes a break. Satan and his demons are relentless at destroying what God is trying to build within His children. You can never let your guard down.

This is why it is imperative that you know the Word of God like the back of your hand! "Watch out! Don't let your hearts be dulled by carousing and drunkenness and by the worries of this life. Don't let the day catch you unaware, like a trap. For that day will come upon everyone living on the earth. Keep alert at all times. And pray that you might be strong enough to escape these coming horrors and stand before the Son of Man."[7]

The ending to this well-known prayer, "For Thine is the kingdom and the glory and the power forever and forever, Amen," is not found in Matthew 6. I searched to see where this phrase is in scripture, and it isn't anywhere. Commentaries mentioned that it was omitted from the King James translation many years ago, but I couldn't find an answer as to why.

The context of this prayer in scripture is found to be a part of Jesus's teaching along with fasting. God is not interested in how much head knowledge you have gained. He is looking for the transformation of your heart. Praying through these steps along with studying scripture will help you to become more like Christ.

Know Scripture Like the Back of Your Hand

Memorizing scripture is another tool that aids in becoming Christlike. This discipline helps ground your heart and mind in Him. Romans 8:38-39 are great verses to memorize. They will help combat the lies that you have believed. "And I am convinced that nothing can ever separate us from God's love. Neither death nor life, neither angels nor demons, neither our fears for today nor our worries about tomorrow, not even the powers of hell can separate us from God's love. No power in the sky above or in the earth below, indeed, nothing in all creation will ever be able to separate us from the love of God that is revealed in Christ Jesus our Lord." Are you convinced? You need daily doses of truth to solidify this reality. Jesus asks His disciples in John 16:31, "Do you finally believe?" He wanted them to really understand who He was and why He came to die for them.

In 1 John 3:1, John says, "See how very much our Father loves us, for He calls us His children and that is what we are. But the people who belong to this world don't recognize that we are God's children because they don't know Him." God is passionately seeking you so that you can know who you are worshiping. He knows you intimately, and He's waiting for you to look to Him. He will make Himself known to you.

His love is consistent and committed, and it requires a commitment from you. You need His help moment by moment to keep such a commitment. As you have seen from Adam and Eve and how history has transpired, man cannot be what God intended without His help. Jesus made the way for you to have His continual help. You have the Holy Spirit living inside of you when Jesus has taken center stage in your heart.

Ponder this: God lives inside a heart that is surrendered to Him. The very God that created the vast universe and has kept over six billion people from destroying His planet, lives within those who have said YES! Doesn't He deserve your undivided attention? Jesus speaks in Luke 12:7, "And the very hairs on your head are all numbered. So, don't be afraid; you are more valuable to God than a whole flock of sparrows." For God to know how many hairs you have on your head, what does that say about His attitude toward you? It says that He cares deeply for you.

My son and I had a conversation on what it will be like when believers are all up in heaven. We think it will be awesome to meet the twelve disciples and ask them what it was like to be with Jesus on earth or to meet Moses, Jonah, Daniel, et cetera. We think that they will be as eager to know from us what it was like to have *God living inside of us while on earth.* We have the better deal, my friends. Let's not squander the gift that lies before us.

Thorns Are No Match for God

Sin causes you to be impaired in one way or another. We all have issues—or thorns, as I call it—that keep us from walking in unity with God. No matter what thorns you carry around, He is always there to show you, change you, and help you to become more holy and set apart for Him. God uses your thorns to remind you that you need God in your life. These irritants keep you humble as they keep you looking up for help. I call them irritants because I am greatly irritated by my thorns.

Paul speaks of this very thing in 2 Corinthians 12:7. It says, "Even though I have received such wonderful revelations from God, to keep me from becoming proud, I was given a thorn in my flesh, a messenger of Satan to torment me and keep me from becoming proud."

Anger and anxiety are my "thorns" that God has used to help me to look up. I had to look up and be willing to be taught by my Father so that I could become what Rob needed as his wife—and eventually become what my children needed as their mother. What in your life has you looking around for help? Look up and you will find what your heart needs. Look up to the One who has remained with you and is patiently waiting for you to recognize His presence. Look up and say, "Create in me a clean heart, O God. Renew a loyal spirit within me."[8]

Psalm 147:5 reveals who God is: "How great is our Lord. His power is absolute, and His understanding is beyond comprehension." He fashioned you in such a way that you can find Him and be known by Him and have understanding. He is amazing, isn't He? I hope by now that you are grasping the love that God has for you and that you have already started the process of restoration and healing.

Ponder this: "The LORD is the everlasting God, the Creator of all the earth. He never grows weak or weary. No one can measure the depths of His understanding. He gives power to the weak and strength to the powerless. Even the youth will become weak and tired, and young men will fall in exhaustion. But those who trust in the LORD will find new strength. They will soar high on wings like eagles. They will run and not grow weary. They will walk and not faint."[9]

Psalm 139 is appropriate for ending our journey together. There are twenty-four verses that reveal who God is and how personal He is with you. His love gives you value and worth. His love heals you. His love enables you to live beyond what you call limitations. His love takes you higher than you can dream, and here's the cherry on top: *you are never alone.*

Let's read Psalm 139, "O LORD, you have examined my heart and know everything about me. You know when I sit down or stand up. You know my thoughts even when I'm far away. You see me when I travel and when I rest at home. You know everything I do. You know what I am going to say even before I say it, LORD. You go before me and follow me. You place your hand of blessing on my head. Such knowledge is too wonderful for me, too great for me to understand.

"I can never escape from your Spirit! I can never get away from your presence. If I go up to heaven, you are there; if I go down to the grave, you are there. If I ride the wings of the morning, if I dwell by the farthest oceans, even there your hand will guide me, and your strength will support me. I could ask the darkness to hide me and the light around me to become night, but even in darkness, I cannot hide from you. To you the night shines as bright as the day. Darkness and light are the same to you.

"You made all the delicate, inner parts of my body and knit me together in my mother's womb. Thank you for making me so wonderfully complex. Your workmanship is marvelous; how well I know it. You watched me as I was being formed in utter seclusion, as I was woven together in the dark of the womb. You saw me before I was born. Every day of my life was recorded in your book. Every moment was laid out before a single day had passed.

"How precious are your thoughts about me, O God, they cannot be numbered! I can't even count them; they outnumber the grains of sand, When I wake up, *you are still with me.* O God, if only you would destroy the wicked! Get out of my life, you murderers! They blaspheme you; your enemies misuse your name. O LORD, shouldn't I hate those who hate you? Shouldn't I despise those who oppose you? Yes, I hate them with total hatred, for your enemies are my enemies. Search me, O God, and know my heart; test me and know my anxious thoughts. Point out anything in me that offends you and lead me along the path of everlasting life."

See how intimate God is with you.

Here is another nugget of truth to keep you going in your journey with the Lover of your soul. Zechariah 14:9 says, "And the LORD will be king over all the earth. On that day there will be one LORD and His name alone will be worshiped." He longs for your love. He longs for your heart to desire Him. Remember 1 John 4:19: "He first loved us."

Romans 5:18-19 is good to remember. It says, "Yes, Adam's one sin brings condemnation for everyone, but Christ's one act of right-eousness brings a right relationship with God and new life for every-one. Because one person disobeyed God, many became sinners. But because one other person obeyed God, many will be made righteous." It's time to live righteous, my fellow sojourners.

You are complete in God. His love for you is everlasting and per-fect. He is waiting to smother you with His love. I want you to know, you will not be disappointed in saying yes to Jesus. I promise you.

A FINAL MESSAGE
CHRIST IS RETURNING

"Look, I am coming soon,
bringing my rewards with me to repay all
people according to their deeds. I am the
Alpha and the Omega, the First and the
Last, the Beginning and the End."
— *Revelation 22:12-13*

Christ returning is the greatest news *next to when He resurrected from the dead.* Jesus is coming back—first for His children, then He will return seven years later to bring judgment upon the earth. Knowing this reality is what keeps you moving forward and helps keep your focus on Him. Like Paul said in I Corinthians 9, you are running the race of faith. The prize is eternal life. Hebrews 13:14 says, "For this world is not our permanent home. We are looking forward to a home yet to come."

God will not leave you in this sinful world. This world, along with Satan, will soon come to an end. As His child, you will live forever in His presence. 1 John 2:15-17 speaks of this so clearly: "Do not love this world nor the things it offers you, for when you love the world, you do not have the love of the Father in you. For the world offers only a craving for physical pleasure, a craving for everything we see and pride in our achievements and possessions. These are not from the Father, but are from this world. And this world is fading away, along with everything that people crave. But anyone who does what pleases God will live forever." *This is important to remember as you walk in faith each day.*

No one knows when Jesus will return. Only God the Father knows. Scripture says that He will come unexpectedly like a thief in the night.[1] You are to live each moment like He is coming at any time. Every day, Jesus comes to take people off this earth. None of us know when our day will arrive, so God wants us ready. At some point, Jesus will return to remove believers all at once. This initiates the start of the final years of life on earth.

Remember when we talked about how Satan used to live in heaven before Genesis 1:1? Well, the best way to describe the story between God and Satan is to think of a court case. God is the Supreme Court Judge, and Jesus is the defense attorney. Because of his lies and deception, Satan was thrown down to earth and given ownership of this world for the time being. He has already been found guilty, but his sentencing hasn't taken place; think of it as house arrest.

We know that courtroom TV shows are very popular. Let's say you are watching one and the show ends with a cliff hanger . . . *to be continued*. This same thing is happening in the heavenly courthouse. Satan is sentenced for his crime, which is rebellion to God. His punishment is death.

Currently, we are living in the *to-be-continued* timeframe. You could call this period the Age of Grace. It is called this because you come to the Father by grace. His grace is revealed through the blood of Christ as He makes you white as snow.[2] As believers, we are anticipating the final episode that will be revealed when Jesus returns.

When He returns, believers in the One true God will rise up to meet Him in the air. Many adults and all children will disappear, leaving many behind to wonder what is going on.

1 Thessalonians 4:15-17 describes what it will be like when Jesus comes back for His Church. "We tell you this directly from the Lord, we who are still living when the Lord returns will not meet Him ahead of those who have died. For the Lord Himself will come down from heaven with a commanding shout, with the voice of the archangel, and with the trumpet call of God. First, the Christians who have died will rise from their graves. Then, together with them, we who are still alive and remain on the earth will be caught up in the clouds to meet the Lord in the air. Then we will be with the Lord forever."

Please note, this is not the second coming of Christ. Jesus will come for His Church first. Believers who are alive on earth during this event will not experience death. One minute you will be walking the dog or driving to work, and the next moment you will be with Jesus along with your brothers and sisters in Christ.

Once His redeemed souls are removed, seven years of tribulation will come upon the earth that will then usher in Satan's sentencing for deceiving man. At the end of these seven years, Jesus will return to judge the earth. This is the second coming of Christ.

God in His mercy and grace instructs you throughout scripture how you are to be living so that you can be prepared for His return. You are a child of the light who is alert, on guard, and wise. You are protected by the armor of faith, wear a helmet of love, and have confidence in receiving salvation from the Lord.[3]

Revelation, the final book of the Bible, gives us a sneak peek into the future, into those seven years that I mentioned earlier. Jesus gave the Apostle John a revelation of the end times for the world. John wrote down what he saw, and you can read about it in Revelation. God wants His children to know and be prepared for what will happen. At the end of the book, I have added a synopsis of Revelation for those who are interested in knowing more about what lies ahead.

A Final Note from Me

I hope you are seeing that God hears your heart. With every beat, He is thinking of you. At the beginning of this book, I asked you what you saw when you looked into the mirror. What do you see now? I hope you are seeing a very loved person—one that is breathtaking. I pray that you and God are getting acquainted and a love story is blooming.

It is important that you receive your salvation from Christ. This is the spark needed to ignite the love between you and God. I want you to take full advantage of the opportunity right now to change your residence from hell to heaven. I hope and pray that my story has ignited a flame inside your heart. Do not ignore it nor put it off until later. Satan will make sure you forget.

I want you to find a place where you won't be distracted or interrupted. Take a deep breath and look up. My sweet friend, I want you to become my sister or brother in Christ. I want to celebrate Christ's love with you forever. Get ready to jump in and be immersed in His redeeming love.

Now, repeat after me, "Heavenly Father, I am scared to let go." Tell God what you are afraid of. There is no need to be shy or ashamed. Do you want in on a little secret? He already knows *every-thing about you.* He is simply waiting for you to tell Him. God is the very safest place to be when you feel vulnerable. I want you to realize this: if God already knows all your secrets and He is still waiting for you with open arms, what does that tell you?

Continue talking to God: "Lord, I screw up—like—a lot, but Your Word says that you love me anyway. I know I am a sinner. I have Adam and Eve inside me. I like apples and I take bites all the time. But no more! I want to live for You. Please come into my heart and heal my brokenness and help me to walk in Your ways. I cannot do this on my own. Thank you for dying for my sins and resurrecting from the dead so that I can have eternal life. I am forever grateful for Your amazing grace and mercy. I do not deserve this, but You say I am worth dying for. Help me to see and understand this crazy kind of love that you have for me. Walk with me, talk with me, and show me through Your Word how to live correctly. Amen."

If you said this prayer with all sincerity, welcome to the family of God. God has begun a great work within you. Read Philippians 1:6. Keep looking up, and He will show you the rest of the way home. All you need to do is trust and obey. You are now an heir to the Kingdom of God. Everything that is God's is now yours, so go and live like the prince or princess that you have become.

I will be praying for you as you deepen your faith in God. May I encourage you to find a Bible-believing church if you don't have one. It is vital to be around other believers. We help each other and build each other up. Get involved in a Bible study. We learn and grow when we study truth with one another. We are created to know truth, God's truth.

Need a place to get started and learn more about God and His Word? Check out my website: United in Love at caroljgerman.com. I write encouragement blogs and Bible studies in an easy-to-read format where you will discover God's amazing love through His Son. You can study two books of the Bible: John and Romans. You will find them under the Learning Truth Blog tab, along with other blogs that will deepen your faith. I will be blogging other books of the Bible as well.

Be patient with yourself and God as He helps you to take on the image of His Son. Salvation is a two-step process. First, you come to believe in Christ as your Savior. Then at some point, you learn to pick up your cross and follow Him—and Jesus becomes your Lord. I had a ten-year span between the two. As I shared earlier in the book, I accepted Christ into my life as a young teen, then ten years later when I got married, I learned to take God at His Word and live it out. I listened to the Holy Spirit.

Faith is a journey, a process, where God leads you by the hand one step at a time. Remember, God will meet you in your daily routine. Look for Him in everything you do. Do not stop trusting and listening to the Holy Spirit. You will have times where you will turn your back on God. Every day you will battle your flesh, but know that God will never leave you. Every day you will wrestle with being a lukewarm Christian. *A lukewarm Christian is someone who has one foot in God and one foot in the world.* You love both God and the world; see 1 John 2:15-17. You have come to know that God wants all of you. He will faithfully lead you back if you look up at Him. Call out to Him, He is there.

Thank you for journeying with me and God. I look forward to spending eternity with you and our Lord Jesus Christ.

DISCUSSION TIME

CHAPTER ONE: WE NEED EACH OTHER

1. What is commitment?

2. Can you relate to any examples of commitment from the chapter?

3. Have you seen how ethnicity, health issues, different backgrounds, and other differences do <u>not</u> stop love?

4. How are commitment and love tied together?

5. How was commitment displayed, or not, in your family?

6. You may have not experienced love and commitment. With God, you have hope. How does this encourage you?

7. Share some memories of your past. What were homes like? Relatives? Holiday times?

8. Why do you think the family unit isn't like it was years ago? What needs to change?

9. How can we show others the same love and commitment that the friends in Mark 2 showed their paralyzed friend?

10. Understand that when love becomes the center, a life quickly adapts and flourishes. How does this encourage you? How can this help you in loving those around you?

CHAPTER TWO: LOVE COMES IN A PACKAGE

1. What do you think about the Trinity?

2. Right and wrong are being challenged:
   a. How important is it to you to "consider the source" when making decisions?
   b. Has technology played a part in the war between right and wrong?
   c. What are the effects to our society when foundational truths are challenged?

3. The Bible is our reliable instructional guide:
   a. How well do you know the Bible?
   b. Did you learn anything new about how the Bible came into being and was written?

4. What did you learn about God the Father? He is committed to loving you, no matter what. How does that make you feel?

5. Have you experienced the Father's love, like Tiffany has?

6. When you realize that God wants you and that He created you, what goes through your mind?

7. What goes through your mind as you realize how small you are compared to the vast universe, knowing that He loves you and that He never stops pursuing you?

8. What did you learn about God the Holy Spirit?

9. We need God. We need to be awakened to His leading and run wild into the future secured by God. Does this excite you or frighten you?

10. You are worth the Trinity's love. You are worth the time they spend loving you. You are worth it. Do you believe this? What will it take for you to believe?

Chapter Three: The Love of Your Life

1. What surprised you about Satan's past?

2. Why was he thrown out of heaven?

3. How would you respond to, "Don't you want to be like God?" How do you act like God?

4. What bait is the enemy dangling in front of you to get your eyes off of Jesus?

5. Did you learn anything new about the sampling of the apple in the Garden?

6. How have you seen God protecting you (like Daniel, Jonah, and the three brothers)?

7. Love is restored when we seek God. Are you interested in seeking Him? To go deeper with Him?

8. Mary and Joseph's life together did not resemble wedded bliss. Could you trust and obey like they did?

9. What did you learn about Jesus that you didn't realize or know?

10. Jesus loves you. Has His love changed you? Do you believe when He speaks and are you willing to obey what He tells you?

Chapter Four: Having Good Intentions

1. It says in Jeremiah 31:33 that a man has it in his heart to follow God. Why then does man struggle?

2. What is sin? Look up verses in the Bible to see what God says.

3. What shortcomings do you have that keeps you defeated?

4. How is God teaching you to depend on Him?

5. What was new about the three temptations that Jesus endured? How does this encourage you to reach out to Jesus, knowing that we are tempted with the very same things?

6. It takes more than just believing to get into heaven—what else is needed? Was this new for you? What needs to change in your life because of it?

7. Describe your life as if you walked obediently. Ask God to help you in the areas you struggle with.

8. How are you encouraged that your past does not deter God from seeking you and wanting to be with you from this day forward?

9. What spoke to you about the ten men with leprosy who were healed and how only one returned to thank Jesus?

10. What comfort do you receive knowing you are safe under His care?

CHAPTER FIVE: UNCONDITIONAL PURSUIT

1. What caused the first murder between two brothers, Cain and Abel? What caused the division between the two brothers Esau and Jacob? Are we any different in our behavior?

2. Is it helpful to realize that we all come from dysfunctional families? How does this help you?

3. Does your life reveal your love for the world or that you love God? What would God have to do in your life to get you to turn to Him?

4. When you are faced with an obstacle or a crisis, where do you go and how do you cope?

5. What causes your foundation to crumble and crack?

6. If God was your norm, what would your life look like?

7. We all are touched by cancer. How has it affected you?

8. What empty chaos is in your life?

9. Fill in the blank. _____ is no match for God! Do you believe this?

10. How has God amazed you?

CHAPTER SIX: MAN'S LAST WORST DAY

1. Have you asked yourself, "How could God do this to me? Why do I have to endure this?"

2. People missed Christ's birth. He was born among the hustle and bustle of daily life. People had their own ideas of what the Son of God would look like. If He came today instead of two thousand years ago, would you know that He arrived? Do you see Him now? He is standing next to you.

3. Jesus invites all: "Come, follow me." What goes through your mind when you read this? Are you willing to follow?

4. How does Christ's resurrection change mankind? How does His resurrection change you?

5. Jesus redeems you. What is your part?

6. I shared why I need saving. What is your story?

7. What are things a believer needs to do to keep on track with God?

8. Eve ate a bite of the apple. How have you taken bites of lies?

9. Do you blame God for things happening in your life? What would happen if you looked at your life from God's perspective and everything you go through could be used for His glory?

10. Today is the day of salvation. Do you desire to know more? God is waiting.

CHAPTER SEVEN: BECOMING MORE LIKE JESUS

1. Is God on the back burner of your life? How's it going for you?

2. What does it mean to you for Jesus to be your Savior? How about Lord?

3. If Jesus is your Lord and Savior, how does your life reflect it?

4. What dumb things have you done that keep you from walking with God? How has it affected your life?

5. My marriage started out in a foreign land. Do you have a foreign-land story, a place that is unfamiliar? God met me. How has God met you?

6. Are you involved in Bible Study? How does being in one help your faith?

7. Waiting is hard. Where is God having you wait? Are you tempted to move forward without him?

8. How are you finishing strong—staying the course? Remember, Jesus is our role model.

9. Are you willing to have a Timothy come alongside you, like Cecilia did for me? Are you willing to be a Timothy for someone else, to encourage and uplift another believer?

10. Are you captivated by God's love?

Chapter Eight: A Heart Transplant

1. Has God spoken to you through His Word? Which verses speak to you and why?

2. Do you have a servant's heart? Jesus came to serve, NOT to be served. Look up Mark 10:45.

3. Is the concept of needing a new heart different for you? How does Ezekiel 36:26 help?

4. Do you take time for God and His Word? What needs to change in your schedule and your mindset for this to become regular?

5. Are you willing to try on some of God's apparel? Discuss Isaiah 61:10? What are some examples of His type of clothing?

6. What would living out Romans 12:2 look like?

7. What are some of your heart's desires? Do you believe God sees and hears you?

8. Has God convinced you of His love? If not, will you let Him?

9. What kind of blinders do people wear that keep them from finding God?

10. Love is for all ages. How does this speak to you?

Chapter Nine: God Is for You

1. How deep of a pit (of sin) did Jesus have to pull you out of?

2. How does the great "I Am" encourage you?

3. God pursues you despite your sin. Is this scary or a relief?

4. How does Adam's response to God when he was hiding, help you to talk to God?

5. God showed me through a handheld game that He hears me. How has He shown you that He is there?

6. The model of the Lord's Prayer is a guide. How does this help you?

7. Memorizing scripture. How would this benefit you?

8. Doesn't God deserve your undivided attention? What do you think your life would look like if you gave it to Him?

9. God lives in a heart that is surrendered to Him. What needs to be surrendered in you?

10. God is for you. How does this affect your life from now on?

The ABCs of Beginning Your Faith Journey with God

If you are wondering how to begin seeking God, below I share what has helped me. Please start out by giving yourself grace as you seek God. I promise, He will reveal Himself in a way that you will know that it is Him. Like anything new, learning to walk with God takes practice. You are developing new habits, ones that will lead you to go deeper with God.

Soon, God will become your safe place, a refuge where you will run to and feel safe and secure. Remember, His presence is what you are seeking and needing. In His presence, you will find rest for your soul.

These simple practices will help you find God and remain in Him as you live out each day:

1. **Read the Bible** every day. I would suggest beginning with the book of John in the New Testament. Then read through the other three Gospels: Matthew, Mark, and Luke. The book of Proverbs teaches how we are to live each day. There

are thirty-one chapters, one for each day of the month. Check out Psalms. Both Proverbs and Psalms are in the Old Testament. Read small portions to start. Remember, it's not how much you read. You are seeking to learn about God and recognize His presence.

2. **Write down** what stands out to you from the Bible. Keep it short and simple. Journal what bothers you in the readings, what makes you happy, etc. You can go back and read what God is showing you. **Keep a prayer journal.** Put a box in front of each prayer. When prayers get answered, you can check the box. I found this helpful in seeing how real God is in my life and in other's lives. Eventually, you will have many checked boxes.

3. **Listen to worship/Christian music**. It is available in all genres. Music that praises God helps to keep your focus on Him.

4. **Memorize scripture**. Take your time and memorize as much as you can handle. A good goal is to learn one verse per week. It is important to have God's Word hidden within your heart.

5. **Pray to God**. Prayer is simply talking to God like you would your best friend. Keep it simple, honest, and real. To help with this, know that God already knows what you need and how He is going to meet your needs. Prayer is for you. It keeps you dependent on Him. You can pray all the time, 24/7. God hears your heart. He knows your unspoken thoughts as well as your audible words. You may have times where you don't know what to say. That's okay. The Spirit intercedes for you as He speaks to God—read Romans 8:26.

6. **Gather with other believers**. Get active at a Bible-believing church. You learn a great deal sharing with other believers. Study God's Word together. It is amazing how much you learn from one another. Take notes when you listen to a sermon. It is helpful to look at the notes throughout your week.

Remember, these six practices are like tools in your toolbox that will keep you walking with God. Be alert to how God is all around you. Look for Him in little things as well as big things. Be thankful in all circumstances and encourage others.

As you walk with God, your faith will grow stronger and you will recognize God more easily. Have patience with yourself and others as you learn to walk with Him. Know that the Holy Spirit walks with you and helps you. Whenever you call out to God, He is there.

UNDERSTANDING THE BOOK OF REVELATION

The Old Testament was under Mosaic Law, also known as the Law of Moses. You read how tedious and difficult it was to follow God, especially for the Israelites. He was preparing them for the Messiah to come and deliver them from their sins. Many prophecies were made leading up to the arrival of the Messiah, which was to be 490 years in the future. When Jesus arrived, 483 of those years had been fulfilled, which means that seven years still have not taken place. Revelation describes these seven years.

You know that the birth of Jesus ushered in the New Testament and that His death and resurrection birthed the Age of Grace. People becoming believers after the resurrection are known as "His Church." Jesus's death and resurrection directly opened the door to God. There was no need for priests any longer, like in the Old Testament. Because of Jesus, you have the Holy Spirit living within you who speaks with God on your behalf.[4]

After reading Revelation, it is evident that there will be a world-wide political power along with a one-world religion. Currently, things are unfolding that indicate that we are heading in this direction.

Revelation 1 sets the stage for earth's final years. Events will take place that Christ wants His servants to be aware of. This final book of the Bible is John's report of what he was shown by heavenly angels. It begins with John writing to seven churches in the province of Asia. Today this is western Turkey. Why God chooses these particular churches is unclear.

Jesus shows John how He has authority over all things. Jesus, the High Priest, is the only mediator between God and man. He has the right to judge sin because He is the divine atonement for sin. The time has come for His long-awaited redemption.

Revelation 2 and 3 teach us about the seven churches. Jesus wanted John to write letters to these churches to give them their report card of how they are doing in serving Christ and serving others. Each report card shows five areas that we can learn from:

1. Jesus tells us who He is. We see that He is the head of the Church. He is the holder of all things and is the First and the Last. He is the resurrected King who has a sharp two-edged sword. He determines what is right and wrong. He has the sevenfold Spirit of God and is holy and true. He holds the key of David and has authority to open and close all things. He is the Amen, the finisher, and completer of all that is His.

2. John gives us a description of each church. We learn that believers represent the Church. His church is not a building where God resides, for God lives within repentant hearts. His children are to be hardworking, to patiently endure trials, to be able to discern false ways, to persevere, and to remain faithful and be loyal to Christ. We are to show love and faith always and be constantly growing deeper in God.

We aren't to be influenced by the world in day-to-day living. We are to adorn ourselves with righteousness, be obedient, and stay strong in Christ.

3. God understands we are human and will stumble. His love and grace lead us to repent and turn back to Him. We see that He is the God of second chances. He never leaves us nor forsakes us.[5]

4. God gives us direction in what to do next. Seven times believers are told, "Anyone with ears to hear must listen to the Spirit and understand what He is saying to the churches." He wants us to pay attention to how we are living the life that He gave us.

5. To those who obey Christ until the end, they will be found victorious and they will receive blessings from God. We are to live serving and loving others while sharing the gospel in word and action. We won't be harmed by the second death, for we will pass through to eternal life with God.

Revelation 4 speaks of the first event that leads up to the second coming of Christ. You will see what true worship looks like in heaven. In the center and around the throne are four living beings that represent traits of God. One of the beings was like a lion, which depicts God as majestic and omnipotent. Another being was like an ox, referring to God as a faithful, patient laborer. The third had a human face, depicting that God

**Heaven is a place of
all-knowing wisdom.**

is intelligent. The last being is an eagle in flight. From this, God's supreme sovereignty over all of creation is clear.

The four beings may represent Christ in the four gospels. In Matthew, Christ is the Lion, the tribe of Judah. In Mark, Christ is the servant of Yahweh, like an ox. In Luke, Christ became the incarnate human. In John, the eagle represents the divine Son of God. Another way to look at it is that the four beings may represent angels who extol the attributes of God.

Whenever the living beings give glory, honor, and thanks to the one sitting on the throne, twenty-four elders fall down and worship Him. They lay their crowns before the throne and say, "You are worthy, O Lord our God, to receive glory and honor and power. For you created all things and they exist because you created what you pleased." You see honor and respect for the One who is King of all kings.

Revelation 5 reveals the second event. John sees a scroll in the right hand of God. There is writing on the inside and outside of the scroll, and it is closed with seven seals. He also sees a strong angel who shouts with a loud voice, "Who is worthy to break the seals on this scroll and open it?" But no one in heaven or on earth or under the earth is able to open the scroll and read it.

Christ steps forward and takes the scroll. He is worthy. You know that Jesus came the first time as the Lamb. Now, He returns as the Lion to judge His creation. The four living beings and twenty-four elders fall down before the Lamb of God. John hears the voices of thousands and millions of angels around the throne and those of the living beings and the elders. Mightily they sing, "Worthy is the Lamb who was slaughtered – to receive power and riches and wisdom and strength and honor and glory and blessing."

Revelation 6 shows us event three. John watches as the Lamb breaks the first of the seven seals. The Lamb has one of the four living beings say with a voice like thunder to each seal, "Come!" Each seal is as follows:

1. **Seal One**: A white horse comes forward. The rider carrues a bow and wears a crown on his head. He rides out to win many battles and gain victory. He is possibly the Antichrist. He has a bow but no arrows, possibly bringing peace for the first three-and-a-half years of the Tribulation. I would guess that this will be a person of great charisma and charm who persuades many people all over the world.

2. **Seal Two**: A red horse comes forward. The rider is given a mighty sword and the authority to take peace from the earth. War and slaughter are everywhere. This horse could represent political power.

3. **Seal Three**: A black horse comes forward. The rider is holding a pair of scales. "A loaf of wheat bread or three loaves of barley will cost a day's pay. And don't waste the olive oil or wine." There will be a high cost for food, which could mean a famine or shortage of food.

4. **Seal Four**: A pale green horse comes forward. The rider is named Death, and his companion is the Grave. They have authority for one-fourth of the earth to be killed by the sword, famine, disease, and wild animals. This could possibly represent the aftermath of war, famine, and disease.

5. **Seal Five**: John sees under the altar the martyred souls of those who stood for the Word of God and for being faithful in their testimony. A white robe is given to each of them. They are told to rest a little longer for their fellow servants

of Jesus will be joining them. This resting time could represent souls that will be saved during the Great Tribulation.

6. **Seal Six**: When this seal is opened, there is a great earthquake. The sun becomes dark as black cloth. The moon becomes red as blood. Stars fall to the earth. Then the sky is rolled up like a scroll and all the mountains and islands move from their places.

Going from a peaceful world to a time of great chaos due to war, slaughter, famine, and disease on a global scale will be terrifying. Adding in great earthquakes and mountains moving positions along with the sun darkening, the moon turning red, stars falling, and the sky rolling up like a scroll will result in the fear of God being so great that people will hide themselves in caves and among rocks of the mountains. They will cry out, "Fall on us and hide us from the face of the One who sits on the throne and from the wrath of the Lamb. For the great day of their wrath has come, and who is able to survive?"

Revelation 7 reveals event four. Here, we see God's people will be preserved. John sees four angels standing at the four corners of the earth holding back the four winds. Another angel comes up from the east carrying the seal of the living God. The four angels have power to harm the land and sea but have been told to wait until the seal of God has been placed on 144,000 of His servant's foreheads. Commentaries don't say exactly who the 144,000 are.

John sees a vast crowd from every nation and tribe and people and language standing in front of the throne and before the Lamb. They are clothed in white robes and holding palm branches in their hands. They signify righteous triumph. Remember when Jesus rode into Jerusalem on a donkey with people throwing palm branches in front of Him before He died on the cross?[6] One of the twenty-four elders told John that these people die in the Great Tribulation.

Revelation 7, 8, and 9 depict events four and five. You see how the first six seals have revealed great destruction and chaos. When the Lamb breaks the seventh seal, there is silence throughout heaven for about half an hour. This particular seal must bring about humbleness, respect, and reverence to hush heaven for that long.

A succession of trumpets is being blown, which signifies the start of judgment.

1. **Trumpet One**: Hail and fire mixed with blood are thrown down to earth. One-third of the earth is set on fire, one-third of all the trees are burned, and all the green grass is burned.

2. **Trumpet Two**: A great mountain of fire is thrown into the sea. One-third of the water in the sea becomes blood, one-third of all living things in the sea die and one-third of all the ships on the sea are destroyed. I looked up how many ships are on the seas at any given time. It was impressive to see a traffic jam of ships.

3. **Trumpet Three**: A great star falls from the sky, burning like a torch. It falls on one-third of the rivers and springs. The name of the star is Bitterness or Wormwood. One-third of the water is made bitter and many die from drinking it. Wormwood is a bitter desert plant which represents sorrow and bitter judgment.

4. **Trumpet Four**: One-third of the sun, one-third of the moon, and one-third of the stars are struck, and they become dark. One-third of the day is dark and also one-third of the night. One eagle cries loudly as it flies through the air, "Terror, terror, terror to all who belong to this world because of what will happen when the last three angels blow their trumpets."

5. **Trumpet Five**: This trumpet brings on the first terror. John sees a star fall to earth. He has been given the key to the shaft of the bottomless pit or abyss. The star is a person, the enemy. Smoke pours out as he opens the shaft. Locusts that look like horses come from the smoke and descend on the earth. Their king is named Destroyer. They can harm only people who do not have the seal of God on their foreheads.

6. **Trumpet Six**: The second terror comes on the scene. John hears a voice speaking from the four horns of the gold altar that stands in the presence of God. The voice tells the angel, "Release the four angels who are bound at the great Euphrates River." Heavenly angels are never bound, so you know that these are demons. These so-called angels who had been prepared for this hour and day and month and year are turned loose to kill one-third of all the people on the earth. John hears that the size of their army is 200 million mounted troops.

John also sees horses with riders. The description of these characters could depict modern warfare. You read that one-third of all the people on the earth are killed by three plagues. With all the death and destruction, people who do not die in the plagues still refuse to repent of their evil deeds and turn to God. You see how mankind has become fearful but that their fear doesn't cause any changes within their hearts.

In **Revelation 10**, John is asked to eat the scroll. "It will be sweet as honey in your mouth, but it will turn sour in your stomach!" When John eats it, that is exactly what happens. The scroll represents God's Word. Jesus is asking John to ingest it. This represents how vital you need to be in believing and obeying God's Word for eternal survival. To believers, His Word will be sweet and comforting. To unbelievers, it may start out sweet but will soon turn sour. This shows that an unbeliever can't receive truth.

Revelation 11 talks about two witnesses. It would be helpful to read Daniel 9:20-27. It is in regard to this time in history. In this passage, the angel Gabriel meets with Daniel and explains to him what John is being shown. Gabriel tells Daniel how much time must pass before the book of Revelation can take place. Be encouraged by the exact detailing and how God has remained faithful from the Old Testament through the New Testament, and will continue to into eternity.

God is committed to us.

John is shown two witnesses who are given power by God to serve as prophets. They are clothed in burlap and prophesy during these 1,260 days. They testify in the midst of unbelief, apostasy, and satanic power. They are a great threat to the entire wicked world for a particular amount of time. When they complete their testimony, the beast that comes up out of the bottomless pit declares war against them and he conquers them and kills them. Their bodies remain in the main street of Jerusalem, the city where Jesus was crucified.

It's hard to fathom how people would get to this point of vileness in celebrating death, but when people's livelihoods are ruined, fear runs amok, and common sense is thrown out the window, you see how depravity and obscured thinking takes a hold of people.

Now, you will learn about the final trumpet of God's judgment upon His rebellious world. The seventh angel blows his trumpet and there are loud voices shouting in heaven, "The world has now become the Kingdom of our Lord and of His Christ and He will reign forever and ever." You will notice that the seventh trumpet isn't completed. It will resume in Revelation 16.

Chronologically, the time is close to Christ's second coming. For now, chapters 12-15 reveal prophecy from another perspective. This period is the second three-and-a-half years of the tribulation. You see a cast of characters: the woman represents Israel, the red dragon is Satan, the male child is Christ, and the archangel is Michael.

Together, we are going to finally be united in love.

Revelation 12 depicts a woman and a dragon. John witnesses two events of great significance in heaven. John sees, in the first event, a woman clothed with the sun and the moon beneath her feet and a crown of twelve stars on her head. The sun represents Israel's future glory. Isaiah 60 talks about this. The twelve stars could be the twelve sons of Jacob. Jacob's son, Joseph, had a dream with this same image. You can find that story in Genesis 37:9-11. The woman is pregnant and cries out because of her labor pains and the agony of giving birth. The birth could represent the emerging nation of Israel in its suffering prior to the second coming of Christ.

In the second event, John sees a large red dragon with seven heads and ten horns along with seven crowns on his heads. His color may represent the bloodshed of all the people. If you go back to Daniel 7:24-25, his ten horns are symbolic of ten kings who reigned simultaneously with the coming world ruler. His tail sweeps away one-third of the stars in the sky and throws them down on earth. He stands in front of the woman as she is about to give birth, ready to devour her baby as soon as it is born.

She gives birth to a son who is to rule all nations with an iron rod. Her child is snatched away from the dragon and brought to God on his throne. The woman flees into the wilderness where God had prepared a place to care for her for 1,260 days. This scene was stated by Jesus in Matthew 24 and in Mark 13 when He was foretelling the future. Matthew 24:12-13 describes the world, "Sin will be rampant everywhere and the love of many will grow cold. But the one who endures to the end will be saved."

Revelation 13 explains the beast that comes out of the sea as well as one that comes out of the earth. John sees a beast rising up out of the sea. This beast is the world ruler, probably a Gentile since the sea represents the sea of humanity. This ruler will have great power to rule and a great hatred towards God. His source comes from Satan himself. It has always been Satan's purpose to receive the worship that is due to God alone. Satan says in Isaiah 14:14, "I will make myself like the most High." You could call it a counterfeit religion. Satan assumes role of God, and the beast assumes the role of Jesus Christ. The whole world marvels at this miracle and gives allegiance to the beast. For forty-two months he is given authority to do whatever he wants.

All the people who belong to this world are commanded to worship the beast. They are the ones whose names were not written in the Book of Life before the world was made. It is vital that you know the words of your Lord and center your life around His foundational truths lest you be taken captive. People dream of a universal religion or church. You will see this during this time in history, but it will not be what you had hoped for. It will be satanic and blasphemous.

As time marches on, Satan's reign is coming to an end.

John sees another beast, one that comes up out of the earth, and it represents a false prophet or religious character whose role is to support the political leader or first beast. What you are seeing here is a false religious system being set up. It imitates the Trinity. Satan masks himself as God the Father. The first beast assumes the place of Jesus Christ, and the second beast, or false prophet, has a similar role to the Holy Spirit. This is Satan's final attempt to substitute a false religion for true faith in Christ.

Satan orders the people to make a great statue of the first beast, who is fatally wounded but then comes back to life. Satan is then permitted to give life to this statue so that it can speak. It commands that anyone refusing to worship it must die.

It is crazy to think that such a thing can give life. It's good to remember that only God can give breath and life, so this could be a robotic or computerized statue that convinces people. Think about how Hollywood can make pretend things look so real on TV and in movies.

The beast requires everyone—small and great, rich and poor, free and slave—to be given a mark on the right hand or on the forehead. No one can buy or sell anything without that mark, which is either the name of the beast or the number representing his name. This is Satan's way of enforcing his control over mankind. ID chips can be implanted. Animals can have chips placed within them so if they get lost, they can be found easier. We have the capabilities for this to happen.

In **Revelation 14,** John sees the Lamb standing on Mount Zion, and with Him are 144,000 who have His name and His Father's name written on their foreheads. I researched some insight into who these 144,000 people are, but no one really knows for sure. The consensus is they are descendants from the twelve tribes of Israel, handpicked by God for a special purpose.

John records how he saw three angels delivering urgent messages from God. It's like He is letting everyone know that the time is arriving for redemption. The first angel carries the eternal Good News to proclaim to people who belong to this world. They represent every nation, tribe, language, and people. "Fear God," he shouts. "Give glory to

Him. For the time has come when He will sit as judge. Worship Him who made the heavens, the earth, the sea, and all the springs of water."

The second angel follows the first angel through the sky shouting, "Babylon is fallen, that great city is fallen, because she made all the nations of the world drink the wine of her passionate immorality." The third angel follows the second angel shouting, "Anyone who worships the beast and his statue or who accepts his mark on the forehead or on the hand must drink the wine of God's anger. It has been poured out full strength into God's cup of wrath. And they will be tormented with fire and burning sulfur in the presence of the holy angels and the Lamb. The smoke of their torment will rise forever and ever, and they will have no relief day or night, for they have worshiped the beast and his statue and have accepted the mark of his name."

Then John hears a voice from heaven saying, "Write this down: Blessed are those who die in the Lord from now on," says the Spirit, "Yes, they are blessed indeed, for they will rest from their hard work; for their goods deeds *follow* them!" Many are mistaken by this. Because of Jesus sacrifice, any good you do is in response to what He did for you. You love because He first loved you.[7]

You will now see the harvest of the earth. John then sees a white cloud, and seated on the cloud is someone like the Son of Man. He has a gold crown on his head and a sharp sickle in his hand. A sickle is referenced as judgment. An angel comes from the Temple and shouts to the one sitting on the cloud, "Swing the sickle, for the time of harvest has come; the crop on earth is ripe." So, the one sitting on the cloud swings his sickle over the earth, and the whole earth is harvested. The last believers on earth are being removed before God's final judgment call.

Revelation 15 depicts the last plagues that will bring God's wrath to completion. John sees God's Tabernacle in heaven thrown wide open. The seven angels who are holding the seven plagues come out.

Revelation 16 shows the rapid succession of events that are more severe and intense than any other event. These events are worldwide, compared to the trumpet judgments which affected parts of the earth at one time.

When you look back at history, there have been storms, diseases, wars, et cetera, and you can definitely see how they are happening with more frequency and how they are getting stronger. The world is in labor, like a woman in labor with her unborn child. The world is groaning and having to deal with birth pains before Christ returns. In Matthew 24, Jesus foretells when the end will come. "Nation will go to war against nation, and kingdom against kingdom. There will be famines and earthquakes in many parts of the world. But all of this is only the first of the birth pains, with more to come."

John describes the bowls of divine wrath being poured out at this time. The first angel pours out his bowl, which leaves horrible, malignant sores on everyone who has the mark of the beast and who has worshiped his statue. The second angel's bowl makes the sea bloody and everything in it dies. The third angel's bowl makes the rivers and springs become like blood also. John hears the angel who has authority over all water saying, "You are just, O Holy One, who is and who always was, because you have sent these judgments."

The fourth angel pours his bowl on the sun, causing it to scorch everyone with its fire. This shows that there will be dramatic climate changes. Everyone is burned by this blast of heat, and they curse the name of God who has control over all these plagues. They do not repent of their sins, turn to God, and give Him glory.

The next angel's bowl reaches the throne of the beast, and his kingdom is plunged into darkness. His subjects grind their teeth in anguish, and they curse the God of heaven for their pains and sores. But they do not repent of their evil deeds and turn to God. This is the last reference for the need to repent.

The sixth angel pours out his bowl, which lands on the great Euphrates River. It dries up so that the kings from the east can march their armies toward the west without hindrance. Kings from the East could mean from the Orient. It's helpful to know that the Euphrates River is the water boundary between the Holy Land and Asia to the east.

John gets a comprehensive view of the preparation of the final bowl of God's wrath. The enemy is unrelenting and isn't giving up easily. Sin is dark and it runs deep.

We finally see Jesus intercepting, "Look! I will come as unexpectedly as a thief! Blessed are all who are watching for me, who keep their clothing ready so they will not have to walk around naked and ashamed." Believers are to be attired in His righteousness, clothing that God Himself supplies. Remember back when you read that we need to get ourselves into God's dressing room and put on clothing that is made by Fruit of the Spirit? People, *it's time to dress for success.* It's time to shower, shave, and get ready for your wedding day with the Groom.

The demonic spirits gather all the rulers and their armies at a place with the Hebrew name *Armageddon.* This is known as the final battle site between the forces of good and evil. Finally, you read about the last angel pouring out his bowl. He pours it into the air and as he does, a mighty shout comes from the throne saying, "It is finished!"

Before the coming of Christ is revealed, chapters seventeen and eighteen give us a detailed description of Babylon, the source of all false religions. They have opposed the faith of Israel as well as the faith of the

Sin is unrelenting. Jesus is the only key to unlocking its deadly power.

church. Babylon is important politically as well as religiously. They are now in their final judgment. Expositors say that these two chapters do not fall chronologically within the scheme of the seals, trumpets, and bowls of the wrath of God. Chapter seventeen seems to fit into the first half of the Tribulation timeframe.

Revelation 17 depicts the great prostitute. One of the seven angels who poured out the seven bowls goes to John and speaks. "Come with me," he says, "and I will show you the judgment that is going to come on the great prostitute who rules over many waters. The kings of the world have committed adultery with her and the people who belong to this world have been made drunk by the wine of her immorality."

There may be an alliance between the Antichrist and the apostate world church of that time. "Together they will go to war against the Lamb, but the Lamb will defeat them because He is Lord of all lords and King of all kings, and His called, chosen, faithful ones will be with Him." This time frame could be the midpoint of the Tribulation. The beast will assume the role of world dictator.

In Daniel 9:27, Daniel states, "The ruler will make a treaty with the people for a period of one set of seven, but after half this time, he will put an end to the sacrifices and offerings. (Side note: seven is set time used in the Bible to reference when Jesus is returning.) As a climax to all his terrible deeds, the ruler will set up a sacrilegious object that causes desecration until the fate decreed for this defiler is finally poured out on him." While he has worldwide political power, he will assume the place of God and demand that everyone worship him or be killed.

Paul explains in 2 Thessalonians 2:4, "He will exalt himself and defy everything that people call god and every object of worship. He will even sit in the temple of God, claiming that he himself is God." The first half of the seven years is characterized by a worldwide church movement which comes to an abrupt end at the midpoint of the seven years. It will be replaced by the final world religion that worships the world ruler.

Revelation 18 describes the last event of the Great Tribulation. "Babylon is fallen, that great city is fallen! She has become a home for demons. She is a hideout for every foul spirit, a hideout for every foul vulture and every foul and dreadful animal. For all the nations have fallen because of the wine of her passionate immorality. The kings of the world have committed adultery with her. Because of her desires for extravagant luxury, the merchants of the world have grown rich." God says, "No more," and allows the plagues to overtake her in a single day. She will be completely consumed by fire for the Lord God who judges her is mighty. In a single moment, all will be gone for the wealthy businesses of the world.

The end of the seven-year tribulation is now at hand. Babylon is no more. You will see the climax of Jesus Christ returning, just as He has promised. You will see a time of victory and rejoicing.

In **Revelation 19**, you see songs of victory in heaven. Heaven is shouting, "Praise the LORD! Salvation and glory and power belong to our God. His judgments are true and just. He has punished the great prostitute who corrupted the earth with her immorality. He has avenged the murder of His servants. Praise the LORD! The smoke from that city ascends forever and ever."

Remember when I mentioned that you needed to be ready for your wedding? The time has come for the wedding feast of the Lamb and you, His bride. His bride is given the finest of pure white linen. This fine linen represents the good deeds of God's holy people. This is the last of fourteen outbursts of praises to God in Revelation.

The angel tells John, "Write this: Blessed are those who are invited to the wedding feast of the Lamb." Those invited to the wedding feast include all the saints since early times. From the beginning of time until this triumphant ending, everything and everyone are to bring Christ glory. God loves to receive all your attention, for He is a jealous God.[8]

You know Jesus's second coming is a prominent focus in scripture. The Bible gives thirty-four references throughout the Old and New Testaments to His return. There is no other god that can boast the title of Resurrected Savior, nor give the promise that he will return to take His children home.

Heaven opens and John sees a white horse standing there. This is the sign of Jesus's coming triumph over the forces of wickedness in the world. Its rider is named Faithful and True, for He judges fairly and wages a righteous war. He has the right to rule, and on his robe is written this title: King of all kings and Lord of all lords.

Next, he sees the beast and the kings of the world and their armies gathered together to fight against the one sitting on the horse and his army. The beast is captured, and with him, the false prophet who did mighty miracles on behalf of the beast. They were miracles that deceived all who had accepted the mark of the beast and who had worshiped his statue. Both the beast and his false prophet are thrown alive into the fiery lake of burning sulfur.

Revelation 20 is a bit confusing, so I used the Bible Exposition Commentary from versebyversecommentary.com. It talks about a timeframe that lasts one thousand years. John sees an angel coming down from heaven with the key to the bottomless pit and a heavy chain in his hand. He seizes the dragon, the old serpent who is the devil, and binds him in chains for a thousand years. The angel throws him into the bottomless pit, which he then shuts and locks so Satan cannot deceive the nations anymore until the thousand years were finished. Afterward, he must be released for a little while.

This will be a time of great blessing for those who choose to believe in Christ. The enemy is finally getting what he deserves. You see two groups of believers. The first group are those whom God resurrected before the Tribulation along with the martyrs who died during these seven years. They will be priests who will reign with Jesus for one thousand years. The second group are the survivors from the Tribulation.

You learn that there are phases to being resurrected from the dead. Christ is the first to arise from the dead. You could call him the First Fruit. The second phase belongs to those who had already died before His resurrection. They arise after Him. Matthew 27:50-53 says, "Jesus released His spirit. At that moment, the curtain in the sanctuary of the Temple was torn in two, from top to bottom. The earth shook, rocks split apart, and tombs opened. The bodies of many godly men and women who had died were raised from the dead. They left the cemetery after Jesus's resurrection, went into the holy city, and appeared to many people."

You and I fit into God's third phase, His Church. Then there are the Tribulation saints and finally the Old Testament saints.

When the thousand years come to an end, Satan will be let out of his prison. He will go out to deceive the nations, called Gog and Magog, in every corner of the earth. Gog and Magog are descendants of Japeth.[9] God was the ruler of Magog the people. They represent rebellion. Read Ezekiel 38-39 to know more about them. You see how Satan is gathering his posse for one last battle. You could say a global conglomerate is gathering together. They will be a mighty army as numberless as sand along the seashore.

Who are those who will follow Satan? They are the survivors of the Tribulation who will enter the Millennium in their natural bodies, and they will bear children and repopulate the earth. Isaiah 65:18-25 references this timeframe. Many will outwardly profess faith in Christ without placing faith in Him for salvation. Even after everything man has been through, man will still choose to follow his own ways rather than follow Jesus.

John sees them as they go up on the broad plain of the earth and surround God's people and the beloved city. This city is Jerusalem, the capital of the world government of Christ. But fire from heaven comes down on the attacking armies and consumes them.

Then the devil, who had deceived them, is thrown into the fiery lake of burning sulfur, joining the beast and the false prophet. There they will be tormented day and night forever and ever.

The final judgment of God is at hand. John sees a great white throne and the one sitting on it. The earth and the sky flee from His presence, but they find no place to hide. He sees the dead, both great and small, standing before God's throne. And the books are opened, including the Book of Life. The dead are judged according to what they had done, as recorded in the books. Notice, there are many books opened, but only one book is needed for believers. The other books are needed for those who walked disobediently. This is humbling to think about. This shows that most people will not be in heaven. People choose the lies of Satan over the truth of Christ.

Revelation 21 and 22, the final two chapters, tell of the new Jerusalem. John was able to witness what we all ponder when we think about what life will be like when the world ends. What will the new heaven and earth be like? He saw our future home. He saw the holy city, the new Jerusalem, coming down from God out of heaven like a bride beautifully dressed for her husband.

Two verses in Isaiah reference the new heaven and earth. Isaiah 65:17 says, "Look! I am creating new heavens and a new earth, and no one will even think about the old ones anymore." Isaiah 66:22 says, "As surely as my new heavens and earth will remain, so will you always be my people, with a name that will never disappear," says the LORD. The new Jerusalem will be permanent.

John then hears a loud shout from the throne, saying, "Look, God's home is now among His people! He will live with them and they will be His people. God Himself will be with them. He will wipe every tear from their eyes, and there will be no more death or sorrow or crying or pain. All these things are gone forever." God's plan has come full circle. Life started out in perfect Eden and now God and man are back together forever.

The one sitting on the throne says, "Look, I am making everything new." Then he says to John, "Write this down, for what I tell you is trustworthy and true." He also says, "It is finished! I am the Alpha and the Omega, the Beginning and the End. To all who are thirsty, I will give freely from the springs of the water of life. All who are victorious will inherit all these blessings, and I will be their God and they will be my children."

John is then taken in the Spirit to a great, high mountain and shown the holy city, Jerusalem, descending out of heaven. He sees no temple in the city, for the Lord God Almighty and the Lamb are its temple. The city has no need of sun or moon, for the glory of God illuminates the city and the Lamb is its light. The nations walk in its light, and the kings of the world enter the city in all their glory. Its gates are never closed at the end of the day because there is no night there. And all the nations bring their glory and honor into the city. Nothing evil is allowed to enter, nor anyone who practices shameful idolatry and dishonesty; only those whose names are written in the Lamb's Book of Life.

One may have many questions on the eternal state that God has prepared for His saints. What we do know from John's description is that it will be a beautiful and glorious future for all who put their trust in the living God. No longer will there be a curse upon anything. For the throne of God and of the Lamb will be there, and his servants will worship Him. And they will see His face, and His name will be written on their foreheads. And there will be no night there, no need for lamps or sun, for the Lord God will shine on them. They will reign forever and ever.

The angel then speaks to John, "'Everything you have heard and seen is trustworthy and true. The Lord God, who inspires His prophets, has sent His angel to tell His servants what will happen soon.' 'Look, I am coming soon. Blessed are those who obey the words of prophecy written in this book.' . . .

"'Look, *I am coming soon*, bringing my reward with me to repay all people according to their deeds. I am the Alpha and the Omega, the First and the Last, the Beginning and the End.' Blessed are those who wash their robes. They will be permitted to enter through the gates of the city and eat the fruit from the tree of life. Outside the city are dogs, the sorcerers, the sexually immoral, the murderers, the idol worshipers, and all who love to live a lie . . .

"The Spirit and the bride say, 'Come' Let anyone who is thirsty come. Let anyone who desires drink freely from the water of life. And I solemnly declare to everyone who hears the words of prophecy written in this book: If anyone adds anything to what is written here, God will add to that person the plagues described in this book. And if anyone removes any of the words from this book of prophecy, God will remove that person's share in the tree of life and in the holy city that are described in this book.

"He who is the faithful witness to all these things says, 'Yes, *I am coming soon.*'"

RESOURCES

Chapter 2

1. Hebrews 13:8
2. Exodus 3:14-15

Chapter 3

1. Ezekiel 28:15
2. Luke 10:18
3. John 4:4-42
4. Luke 19:1-10
5. John 19:30
6. Genesis 7:11-12 and Hebrews 11:7

Chapter 5

1. Romans 8:1
2. Genesis 4:7
3. James 1:17
4. Hebrews 4:13

Chapter 7
1. Genesis 17:15-16
2. Genesis 17:1-6
3. Genesis 16:2

Chapter 8
1. 2 Corinthians 10:3-5

Chapter 9
1. Hebrews 4:16
2. Psalm 145:1-3
3. Hebrews 9:28
4. Matthew 28:18
5. Matthew 6:26
6. 1 John 1:9
7. Luke 21:34-36
8. Psalm 51:10
9. Isaiah 40:28-31

Christ's Returning
1. 1 Thessalonians 5:2
2. Isaiah 1:18
3. 1 Thessalonians 5:4-8
4. Romans 8:26-27
5. Hebrews 13:5
6. John 12:12-13
7. 1 John 4:19
8. Exodus 34:14 and Deuteronomy 4:24
9. Genesis 10:2

NOTE: The content of Pastor Claussen's sermon has been used with his permission.

Nuggets of Truth to Keep You Encouraged

From Chapter One:

Serving is the key to commitment and love.

When one receives the proper care, one blooms as he is intended and brings joy to others.

We need each other.

You belong, even though you are not perfect.

When you are willing to change, grow, and mature, something beautiful happens.

From Chapter Two:

Love gives room for expression, even if it grieves the Creator.

Seek a source that can teach you how to live properly so that everyone benefits.

Sin causes us to toil through life with free will on our back.

From Chapter Three:

Life will now become a labor of love (the result of sin).

God loves His people to the point of risking Himself.

His eye is always upon me.

From Chapter Four:

We can't afford <u>not</u> to know scripture.

We are like sheep, and we need a shepherd to guide us.

It is within us to seek and find God.

Satan is playing a very destructive game with us.

From Chapter Five:

Sin disrupts love.

Sin does not deter His love.

We won't heed either when our lives follow what the world dictates.

Even in the darkest corners of this world, He is there with you.

His is a crazy love that defies circumstances.

From Chapter Six:

The offering of Himself is the greatest sacrifice of love and commitment.

God's commitment was to send His Son to conquer death and redeem us back to Himself.

Jesus won me over with His love.

You possess a worthiness that will make this world better.

From Chapter Seven:

When God speaks, you can be sure that it will come to pass.

He has a process of helping us to let go of ourselves and become more like Jesus.

You have to see the truth of who you are in your sinful, earthly condition before God's healing love can penetrate and heal you.

View your relationships in the light of who God is and how He loves you.

Be captivated by God's love.

From Chapter Eight:

When you are making your own decisions, in your own way, for your own life, you live in rebellion against who you are made to be.

I needed a new heart and God gave me one when I called on Him.

He reminds me of what is of utmost important, His Presence.

As I sought God and learned from Him, I was finding that He not only answered my prayers, but He answered my heart's desires.

From Chapter Nine:

He is unwavering in His pursuit of His children.

He loves and cares about us imperfect people.

God is so passionately seeking each of us so we can know, for sure, who He is so that we will recognize who we belong to, and we will want to live accordingly.

Life on earth is preparation for living in His Presence.

ABOUT THE AUTHOR

The love that God has shown Carol is what fuels her to encourage others through writing. She wants to share His love with everyone around her. When she is not writing, she enjoys spending time with family and friends. She has been married to her woodsy warrior for over thirty years, and they have raised two children, one of whom is now married. She enjoys a variety of activities, like traveling, biking, and hanging by a bonfire. She loves animals, doing arts and crafts, and riding roller coasters. She resides in Minnesota where she enjoys the four seasons.